# Soccer Coaching
# Development and Tactics
### *By Andrew Caruso*

*Edited by*
*Richard Diedricksen*

# Dedication

This book is dedicated to all the volunteers who have contributed time and resources to *The Great Game*, but especially those who remember WHY they got involved.

You have made this revision possible through your many purchases.

# *Acknowledgements*

Richard Diedricksen through his organizational skills, editing, patience, and soccer knowledge took the mass of content and gave it maximum meaning.

Many thanks for the thousands of requests from U.S. Soccer Coaches, Physical Education Programs, Soccer Administrations for the <u>Suggestions for a Typical Effective Practice—Youth Coaches Guide</u> which provided the encouragement for the book.

Special thanks to Art Lemery who encouraged the early manuscripts. Also Bobby Clark, Gary Palmisano, Rich Broad, John Cossaboon, Bob Dikranian, Mike Freitag, Tom Gibbons, Doug May, Ray Perez, Sue Ryan, Irv Schmid, Tim Schum, Eric Swallow, Chris Sweeney (my avowed mentor), Jeff Tipping, Jerry Yeagley, and Anson Dorrance.

Thanks are in order to my wife, Eva. Thanks also to my son, Troy, and my daughter, Janine, who helped me learn about youth development in sports and their respective sports of basketball and soccer.

Tom Gibbons brought me back to the great game. Joel Jacko, Ken Gableman, Gran Roe, Barry Kasven nurtured my early efforts.

Thanks are in order to Joan Lange with whom I had the pleasure of helping shape the writing program in the Brentwood Public Schools; in so doing, she helped me grow. Both Kwik Goal Ltd. (my brother, Vincent, its founder) and the Brentwood Public Schools contributed opportunities and confidence for such an undertaking.

To Huntley Parker, my coach at Brockport State College, I owe so much, for it is he who gave the model of positive coaching. Thad Mularz, my high school coach and hero, caused me to play soccer and continue my education.

My mother, father, and my grandmother helped by providing unlimited love...no restrictions and no parameters. It seems without this, success even if attained is without joy.

The Long Island Junior courses, the National Soccer Coaches Association courses, Wiel Coerver and no less than 150 plus clinics helped to form the foundation concepts.

The players of my Celtic Team, my fellow coaches who corrected and listened.

The grass roots soccer club meetings and clinics throughout the U.S. crystallized the thoughts presented.

Typists Marion Sidoto, Joan Clarkson, Paula DePaul, and Lisa Habl endured my crude manuscripts.

Thanks to all who published my many articles.

Special thanks to Kimberly Bender Kentwell for enduring this revision.

Thanks to the many unmentioned contributors who have also been infected with *The Great Game*.

# Table of Contents

# Forward - The Great Game

Before the turn of the century, twenty million Americans will be playing the great game of soccer. This guide is for their coaches; it will help both the new and the experienced youth and high school coaches develop complete players, those who master the three fundamental elements of technique, tactics, and function. There are many technique books on the market, and a few tactical books, but none which attempt to **integrate** technique, tactics, and function. As in state-of-the-art coaching for all sports, this integration is best developed through a system of progressions. Building upon a logical progression of exercises, drills, and shortsided games, this guide will show the youth coach how to apply the principles of play to the game of soccer and the development of soccer players. Too often these principles are overlooked by coaches; yet they are the very foundation of the game!

This book is the culmination of a lifetime of soccer experience as player, fan, coach, author, clinician, licensing instructor, and designer of equipment. While it remains true that the game itself is the best teacher, the best coaches also learn from licensing courses, clinics, videotapes, books, observation, and conversation. This book owes something to each of these sources. It shares the vision of American soccer as seen by the United States Soccer Federation, the National Soccer Coaches Association of America, and top youth, high school and college coaches across the nation, whose contributions to the game and to this book are invaluable.

Inexperienced youth coaches should read the appendix (esp. Suggestions For A Typical Effective Practice) before reading Chapters 1-13.

May your love of the great game of soccer ever increase, and may this adventure contribute to your knowledge and enjoyment.

# Introduction
# Principles of Coaching

The youth coach should weigh the relative importance of four main objectives for any soccer program: player development, fun, participation, and sportsmanship. A sound program should allow for all four objectives, and if winning means more than any of these, the coach should avoid youth coaching. The key word for youth practice sessions is...FUN! If your players had fun, chances are you ran a good training session. If they did not have fun, you may have covered too much, taken some short cuts, or coached above or below them. Competitive practice games are usually fun, and can embody anything you want to teach. With variety, full participation, and positive reinforcement, you can maintain motivation and fun. Not to be confused with silly behavior, fun comes from an involvement in learning which depends on a level of activity appropriate to the players' needs; fun also comes from accomplishment, as in a progression to higher levels of play.

Participation directly relates to fun. Most kids would rather be actively playing on a team that goes 3 and 7 than sitting on the bench for a team that goes 7 and 3. But participation is even more important in practice! Good coaches ensure participation by avoiding inactive waiting lines in drills, and by insisting that each player have a ball of his own whenever appropriate. The regular use of 1v1 and shortsided games, with 2 to 6 players per side, dramatically increases player involvement as well as development; therefore smallsided games are absolutely essential for all levels, but especially the younger players. No soccer country in the entire world starts its youth players with 11-a-side games!

Development is an aspect of coaching that is often

misunderstood by well-intentioned coaches. Development is concerned with the emotional growth and physical skill of the individual player, rather than the record of the team. We would do well to remember that not every team and not every kid is capable of world class levels of play. Our task is to help young players become as good as **they** can be, and want to be. We are dealing with kids, not professional athletes. Your players will respect you for the person you are long after they have forgotten the season's won-lost numbers. A sound program adjusts these objectives according to the needs of the players, not the coaches! The younger the player, the greater the emphasis on fun. But even high school players need a certain amount of enjoyment. Good coaches find the balance that keeps a healthy perspective on fun, participation, development and sportsmanship.

Good coaches also must find the balance in all four components of any game, which must be adjusted according to the player's individuality. The first is **psychological**, which does not need to be all that complex. Suffice it to say that kids need fun, variety, and encouragement. They do not need to be criticized nor told what to do every time they get the ball. The second component is **fitness**; players can develop fitness by working with a ball, developing skill alone or in small groups instead of running laps and doing routine exercises. The activities in this book will develop fitness for your youth players. The third component is **technique**; this refers to the basic skills of soccer: shooting, dribbling, heading, passing, receiving, and tackling. Development of technique requires time and repetition. The fourth component is **tactics**; these are the thinking and decision-making aspects of the game, such as what to do and where to go with and without the ball. Shooting is a technique; deciding when, where, and how to shoot is a tactic.

How does the coach deal with all these components within the confines of a single practice session? First, the psychological aspect is best handled by being positive, and by asking rather than telling, i.e. "Where should the standing foot be when passing?" Fitness, technique, and tactics can be incorporated into a system called "**Economical Training**," which incorporates two or more of these components into a  single activity. With the drills and smallsided games outlined in this guide, players can develop any skill at the same time they are learning tactics and/or improving fitness. Good coaching, however, concentrates on only one aspect of the game per practice.

Teaching the basic skills in soccer requires time, patience, and imagination. To get the maximum number of touches on the ball, each player must have a ball. Each skill is best taught using the established progression of fundamental, game-related, and game condition drills. Teach only one skill per session. At the fundamental stage, the skill is demonstrated, key points are briefly explained, and time allowed for sufficient practice and correction. There is no pressure on the players, no defender, and little movement. When players can execute the skill, the coach can progress to the match-related stage; that is, some movement and defensive pressure is added (up to 40% for each). As soon as the skill can be successfully executed at this level, move on to the match condition stage; gradually increase the speed and defensive pressure to actual game conditions. Make up a game that will allow the players to repeatedly perform the selected skill. This approach will incorporate the given skill into real game conditions, as well as motivate the players more than drills. The following chapters will suggest progressions that are fun, practical, and proven successful with players of all ages and abilities.

The activities in this book use the progression concept not only to develop technique, but also to develop tactics. Many coaches believe that no amount of tactical knowledge will make up for poor technique. Therefore, they neglect to develop their players' tactical knowledge. We need to teach both technique and tactics! Players can be tactically sophisticated without great technique, and vice versa!

The major confusion is between individual and team tactics. Too often players are not helped to decide when and where to dribble, pass, shoot, shield, nor how to do a 1-2 move, takeover or overlap and yet the coach is attempting team tactics, positional instruction and team formations, elaborate game plans etc. From the first moment at age 5 in a 2v2 there are many little important decisions THAT CAN NEVER BE SEPARATED FROM TECHNIQUE.

While there is some truth to the idea there are no tactics without technique a better statement is we can never separate technique from decisions - - playing soccer involves both, OR IT IS NOT SOCCER!

In good practice sessions and smallsided games, technique, tactics, and functional roles are developed **simultaneously;** however, coaching involves a logical order of instruction in focusing on a single aspect at a time. Ideally, when we teach young players, we must integrate technique with tactics, and then move on to function, which refers to either a particular position or an area of a field (i.e., fullback, defensive third). Realistically, this is too much material to cover in a single season, especially for beginning players, who need time to develop technique. Under the pressures of time and the winning ethic, many youth coaches make the mistake of advancing from technical training directly to functional training, thus by-passing the tactical stage. This strangles both technical and tactical development because it limits the all-important stage of making and carrying out decisions. The result is a deadly game where fullbacks often stand idle, occasionally clearing the ball with aimless kicks. To develop young players, we need to concentrate on technique and related basic individual and small group tactics. Simply stated, teach your players how to play soccer; then, and only then, teach them how to play specific positions! Even if you never get to functional training, you will have set the proper foundation.

Of course, the priorities for young players are ball control, collecting, dribbling, basic passing and receiving, and short-sided work requiring much ball contact and decision-making. But before there is any concern for positioning, team arrangements, or team tactics, the coach should teach the PRINCIPLES OF PLAYER ROLES in soccer, upon which all tactics must be understood! Discussions of formations (5-3-2, 4-4-2, etc.) are academic and futile without the basic knowledge of first, second, and third attackers and defenders and their roles in the game. Once a player has a reasonable feel for the ball so that she can receive, dribble, pass, and shoot, she is ready to learn these basic principles of player roles. Even average players as young as eight years can begin to implement these concepts, which can be refined over an entire playing and coaching career. Players need not know the names of roles, nor be able to explain them; but they do need to use these concepts, though their knowledge may be mostly intuitive.

Young players will never learn roles in 11v11, so we must play much 1v1, 2v1, 3v3, 4v4, etc., in order for players to master penetration, support, mobility, delay, cover and balance. Without this knowledge no team arrangement is effective and with players who understand these basics of soccer any system will work!

The principles of player roles can be demonstrated using six players, three attackers and three defenders. Any team on attack must have:

> 1. a first attacker (player about to receive or in possession of the ball) whose job it is to penetrate or at least draw a defender;
> 2. a second attacker who gives support;
> 3. third attackers (there may be more than one) who provide mobility.

Any team defense must have:

> 1. a first defender whose job is to apply pressure to the ball and delay the attack;
> 2. a second defender who offers cover (help for the first defender);
> 3. third defenders who balance and concentrate the defense.

Note a simple example of all three offensive and defensive roles in diagram that follows:

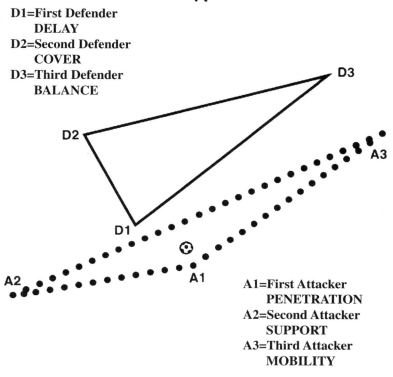

**D1=First Defender**
    **DELAY**
**D2=Second Defender**
    **COVER**
**D3=Third Defender**
    **BALANCE**

**D3**

**D2**

**A3**

**D1**

**A2**

**A1**

**A1=First Attacker**
    **PENETRATION**
**A2=Second Attacker**
    **SUPPORT**
**A3=Third Attacker**
    **MOBILITY**

The older term delay is used instead of pressure on the ball because this is a major weakness of youth soccer in the U.S.

These principles will be developed throughout this book to enable the coach to build a working knowledge of basic soccer, to foster quality player development and to devise intelligent individual and team tactics. The first chapter will fill out the skeletal diagram with the vital information about the principles of play, which are simple to understand, to teach and to apply to every aspect of the great game of soccer!

# *Key*

——————————————▶  Player Run

– – – – – – – – – –▶  Path of the Ball

∧∧∧∧∧∧∧∧∧∧∧▶  Player Dribbling

# 1

# *The Principles of Player Roles in Soccer*

The basic principles of soccer deal with the contrast between attack and defense. Attack begins the instant a team is about to or has gained possession of the ball. The responsibilities of the attacking team involve three major roles, which we call first, second, and third attacker. The FIRST ATTACKER (A1) is the player in possession of the ball or about to receive the ball, regardless of his position on the field. A1's main responsibility is PENETRATION; that is, to get the ball behind the defenders. If within scoring range, the first objective is to score a goal. Otherwise he will try to move the ball forward with dribbling or a penetrating pass. A1 attempts to get the ball to the most dangerous location possible. The mental responsibility of A1 may be the easiest, but penetration is the single most difficult skill in soccer, requiring excellent technique. Imaginative, skillful dribbling and shielding, accompanied by deft passing, are difficult and important.

The first attacker becomes much more dangerous when a SECOND ATTACKER (A2) creates quality SUPPORT, thus giving the attack the width it needs to be effective. This gives A1 more options. A2 can generate penetration by receiving a pass (thereby be coming A1), or by drawing a defender away. A2 is most effective when she forces a defender to commit either to marking her or covering a space, but not accomplishing both. A2's main responsibility is to ensure possession, by always being ready to receive A1's pass, either to the feet or to space. Generally supporting from a position diagonally behind the first attacker, A2 offers quality support. She must, always, be ready to become the first defender if the ball is lost. There may be several THIRD ATTACKERS (A3), whose job is to create MOBILITY by disturbing the defense through positioning and running diagonally or across the field. These movements are designed to get behind and spread the defense. Often working with other third attackers, A3 draws the defenses attention and disturbs its balance. This creates openings or passing lanes for the first attacker. In youth soccer, third attackers may tend to be stationary because they do not always feel involved in the play, esp. in 11 aside. At higher levels, third attackers make many runs which do not reward them with a pass, yet they help the attack immensely by creating space and confusing the defense. The role of the third attacker is the most complex of the attacking roles and does not need to be stressed with the youngest players.

A sophisticated offense requires a worthy defense if it is to develop further. Therefore, once players have developed confidence in individual and small group usage of the ball, then and only then do we begin teaching defensive roles. Like the attacking roles, there are three roles of defense, which begins the moment possession of the ball is lost. Often it begins when a player anticipates possession will be lost.

The FIRST DEFENDER (D1) is the player who marks the first attacker. The major responsibility of the first defender is to DELAY the attack and put pressure on the ball. It is important to note that D1's first priority is not to immediately attempt to win the ball through aggressive play or tackling. The essence is to slow down or stop penetration, whether by pass, dribble or shot. The first defender protects the goal by staying goal side of A1. He must be patient; once there is cover (a second defender to assist him), he may attempt to win the ball. He may try to steer A1 away from a dangerous area, or he may force A1 to make a square or backward pass. D1 is successful when he prevents penetration in any form; that is:

1. He delays A1 until defensive cover (D2) arrives;
2. He wins the ball;
3. He prevents A1 from turning towards goal or looking up;
4. He forces A1 to make a poor pass;
5. He forces A1 to make a square or backwards pass;
6. He forces A1 to shield or dribble across the field or backwards

Alternatively, D1 is unsuccessful when he allows A1 to penetrate in any way (dribble forward, pass forward, or shoot). Where D1 is defending against two attackers, he is successful when the defense recovers to a two-versus two, or better.

The SECOND DEFENDER (D2) is usually the next closest to the ball after D1. The role of second defender involves several responsibilities, but foremost is to offer COVER for D1. This means his first job is to assist D1 by positioning himself at a correct angle behind D1 and communicating with him (such as telling him when to tackle). This provides depth for the defense, and forces A1 to deal with two defenders. D2's second role is to mark A2, but he cannot mark him so closely as to deny cover for D1. In fact, he may invite a pass from A1 to A2, but if this is a square or backwards pass, D2 is successfully doing his job. The second defender must play a space, a man and the ball simultaneously, as well as use the off-side law to his advantage. All this requires vision, but many young players develop an intuition for this role. D2 is successful when he provides good cover for the first defender. If A1 beats D1 or passes to A2, D2 must be ready to become the first defender.

As in the attacking roles, there may be several THIRD DEFENDERS (D3), who add CONCENTRATION and BALANCE to the defense. They accomplish this by staying goal side of the player they mark, restricting space, providing tight marking in the vital area, and communicating. All defenders must work hard when the ball is moving. Third defenders may mark an attacker, cover a space, or both. Thus this role can become too complex for the beginner. The youth player needs to know only the basics of this role: mark a man or cover a space to keep the attack from entering a dangerous area. Note a more detailed example of all three offensive and defensive roles is shown here.

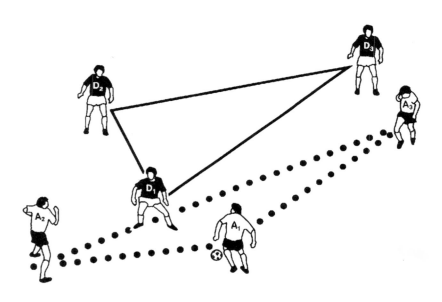

**Diagram #1: This is the foundation for understanding 11v11 team play.**

A1 will try to penetrate. Note A2 has excellent opportunity to receive (support). A3 is allowing for a long pass (mobility), but definitely keeping D3 from A1.

**A1 = First Attacker**

*(player about to receive or in possession of ball)*

**PENETRATION**

*(Main responsibility is to get behind defenders)*

• Score if possible
• Forward movement preferred
• Get ball to most dangerous location possible
• Take chances to score
• Becomes much more dangerous when a 2nd attacker offers quality support and 3rd attacker truly provides mobility
• Confident ball handlers with excellent dribbling skills make very dangerous first attackers creating enormous problems for the defense.

**A2 = Second Attacker**

*(Try to insure possession)*

**SUPPORT**

*(Focus is possession)*

• Generally behind ball and open to receive ball
• Confuse second defender, do not allow him to cover and mark
• Always ready to receive—at feet or in space
• Be ready to be first defender if ball is lost
• Communicate to first attacker

**A3 = Third Attacker**

*(Disturb defense through positioning)*

**MOBILITY**

*(Width and depth)*

• Get open to receive ball (constantly check away & to ball)
• Draw defender's attention
• Work with other third attackers
• Get behind and spread defense
• Maintain eye contact and accelerate to receive
• There can be several third attackers
• Diagonal runs, overloads, occupy dangerous locations, etc.

**D1 = First Defender**

*(Covers first attacker)*

**DELAY**

*(Pressure on ball carrier)*

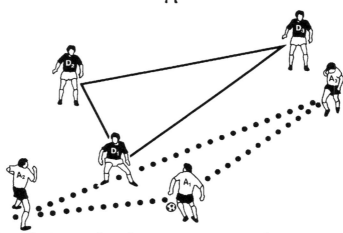

- Be patient; once there is cover, more aggressive moves to win ball are made
- Attempt to steer player to sideline or a helping teammate
- Protect goal, stay goal side
- Force square or back passes
- Win ball, go for ball or tackle when you have cover
- Keep attacker from turning and looking up

**D2 = Second Defender**

*(Helping first defender)*

**COVER**

*(Focus is double coverage)*

- Cover precedes man coverage, do both as best as possible, but cover is first priority
- Provide DEPTH
- Attempt to cut out passes
- Be ready to be first defender, stop shots and dangerous passes
- Maintain a space; see ball and man
- If the ball is won do something contructive

**D3 = Third Defender**

**BALANCE**

*(Concentration)*

- Restrict space; squeeze attacking space
- Cut out passes when attempt is safe
- Stay goal side and talk (communicate)
- Always recover to the penalty spot unless behind it
- Always attempt to see ball and man
- There can be several third defenders

## Diagram #2: Aggressive Support

Here there is still support (A2) and mobility (A3), but the total posture is more aggressive in terms of penetration, since both receivers are in front of the ball. Following the **first law of attack**, the team in possession is **spreading** out and therefore using a larger area. The defense, on the other hand, follows its **first law**, which is **concentration**. They therefore occupy a smaller area.

Teaching the responsibilities of these player roles might be done in a 3v3 activity, but 4v4 might be better for experienced players. In a 20 by 30 yard grid, the coach can walk the players through a demonstration, briefly explaining how the roles change as the ball is passed. Bear in mind that development of a single role may take two to five sessions. Furthermore, only 20-30 minutes a session can be devoted to direct teaching of these roles, because all teachings must be placed into a progression leading up to match condition. Explanation and demonstration must take less than three minutes. After the walk through demonstration, the coach may have a 3v3, 4v3, or 4v4 shortsided game in the grid. The coach would use 'freeze' commands: at the command "Freeze!" or the whistle, all players immediately stop where they are. The coach explains where selected players are supposed to be and why. Play continues. Even though errors may occur every 15 seconds, the coach usually allows continuity of play to develop, and only stops play every two minutes or more. Only during the freeze does the coach talk to the group. Coaching points for individuals can be made as play continues, but talk is not continuous.

From here this exercise could progress in any of several directions, depending upon the coach's objective for the practice. (Each practice should focus on a single skill and related tactic, and always progress through the fundamental, match-related, and match condition stages to as realistic a game as possible, adapted to the particular skill and tactic of that session). For example, goalkeepers and/or goals could be added to afford realistic shooting and goalkeeping practice (you might need to enlarge the grid). Another approach would be to impose specific limitations on the players, such as not allowing A1 to try to penetrate unless she has good support from A2. These adaptations would focus on each of the offensive and defensive roles, **one role per session**. Other limitations could focus on technique, such as left foot only, or two-touch only. The possibilities are endless, and the coach will soon be able to devise her own adaptations to achieve the desired result. The next chapters will show you how to use these principles in specific progressions to develop your players in every aspect of the game.

# 2

## *Dribbling and Development of the First Attacker*

The youth coach should focus on player development which is greatly dependent upon the ability to dribble the ball. Of course, there is a place for one touch soccer; but there is a greater need for players developing confidence with the ball prior to one touch. In order not to kick the ball away mindlessly when there is no available pass, first attackers must be able to dribble and shield. Since every player becomes the first attacker as soon as she receives the ball, every player, even the goalie, needs to develop dribbling skill. Exciting dribbling, such as a series of 1v1's, is a highlight of the game.

Great players are able to penetrate with the ball or possess when either is required. While nearly all the immortals of the game were excellent dribblers, most relied on one or two good moves which they used repeatedly. However, the way to develop good dribblers varies greatly from **being one**. Developing good dribblers is not simply teaching one or two moves; teaching dribbling involves training players to perform many moves; then, and only then, can they choose the few that work best for them. Besides, when you teach dribbling there is much ball contact which automatically enhances total ball control.

Dribbling is the most individual, creative, and expressive skill in soccer. There may be no "wrong" way to dribble, but there are general characteristics of good dribbling. These include keeping the ball under close control, even to the point where the ball is sometimes under the player (Cruyff move); touching the ball with almost every step taken; using both feet, and also the various surfaces of each foot, including the inside, outside, sole, rear, and instep; going in either direction with a particular move; keeping the head up enough to see both the ball and the field; changing direction sharply, quickly, and frequently, if necessary; changing speed, with stops, slow deliberate movements, rapid acceleration from dribble to drive, and rapid deceleration from drive to dribble; and most important, using a variety of well-executed feints.

Dribbling development helps players build confidence and poise. The physical requirements are flexibility, fast footwork and thousands of touches on the ball in practice and game conditions. While flexibility varies from player to player, it can be maximized through proper stretching and practice with the ball. Flexibility allows the player to get very low and explode away with speed using a power move. The power move begins with a low crouch or boxer's stance over the ball, with the player gradually rising to an upright position as speed is attained. Fast footwork is developed when good technique is combined with rapid and numerous repetition, which calls for literally hundreds of touches per practice session. This is not nearly as difficult as it may sound! Infact, good training sessions require approximately a thousand touches per session.

There are dozens of moves, which can be joined together in innumerable ways, thus creating a dribbler's unique style. Although many of these moves can be named (scissors, sole roll, pulling the V), players need not learn them by name. Over the course of a season, the coach should introduce many moves to the players; if he cannot demonstrate, he should find someone who can. Often players can teach each other their favorite moves. Bear in mind that every player will not make use of every move; it is enough that each player find the two or three moves that work for her. As the coach, teach players to go both ways from a given move, and to gain some "ambi-footness" from the exercises. Require flexibility and an explosive getaway. To do this, players should bend their knees to lower their center of gravity.  Here then is a workable progression for teaching the technique of dribbling. First of all, dribbling can be an integral part of the warm-up. For the youngest players, juggling a balloon is a great exercise: it puts everything in slow motion, to help develop coordination and touch. With older players, juggling a soccer ball (especially reduced inflation) develops touch and is a good warm-up component. Allowing the ball to bounce between juggles is another helpful step before full-scale juggling, and is especially helpful in loosening the hips. The inside and the outside of the foot can be used more easily when a bounce is employed. Competent jugglers should work from left to right and right to left, high to low and low to high body parts, then add movement and change of direction. Instead of stopping whenever the ball hits the ground, players should explode away and change direction with the ball the instant it touches the ground. Collection and lifts can be developed at the same time. These approaches are much more valuable than simply trying to keep the ball in the air with random touches or a single body part used repeatedly.

The next activity for all age players is dribbling in a confined area, which forces them to look up in order to avoid collisions. The basic tactic involved here is to slow down in traffic, and speed up in open space. Beginners often do the opposite. The coach can then add specific demands - left foot only, outside of foot, change direction or speed on whistle, shielding whenever close to another player. The coach can evaluate his players during this time, so he knows what to emphasize in the instruction. Meanwhile, the players are getting a practice and a warm-up, especially if they alternate stretching with the dribbling exercises. Now they are physically and mentally ready to learn more.

Teach them a few moves, maybe just one or two in a given session. However, do four or five of the moves previously learned. As in all technical instruction at the fundamental stage, it is best to start with a clear and brief demonstration. Then have each player work on the move with a still ball and no opposition. (Every player should have a ball for these sessions.) Next practice the move with a very slow moving ball and no defender. A guide line for introducing a move is 50 repetitions, which can be accomplished in less than three minutes.

As success is achieved, progress to the game-related stage by working with a slightly faster moving ball, token pressure, and shielding whenever close to another player. Work up to the game condition (grid) stage by increasing the defensive pressure and speed, then make a game of it. Add small goals or use a ball, cone, or player with his feet spread for a goal. Keep score, not necessarily by the number of goals, but perhaps by the number of times the move is executed. Another approach would be to reinforce dribbling moves in shortsided games: give points for usage of particular moves or correct shielding (side-on), or demand that before the ball is passed, a move must be used.

A highly successful method for combining many touches with developing specific moves is to dribble the ball back and forth between the insides of the feet three times (the ball goes back and forth, not forward) then immediately execute the move. The odd number of touches between the insides of the feet ensures that the move is developed with each foot. From here, the activity progresses to more movement and increasing defensive pressure, then to shooting opportunities and smallsided games which focus on dribbling.

When players are in development, a good practice involves many touches of the ball. Coaches should include at least ten minutes of dribbling practice per session, and of course, much more when dribbling is the focus of the practice. When your practice session focuses on dribbling, here is a good way to get one or two thousand touches of the ball in the first thirty minutes of practice. A touch a second can be accomplished in this kind of activity, which offers far more variety than simply dribbling aimlessly throughout the field. Spend a few minutes at each of the following, and incorporate shielding wherever practical:

- Each player with a ball, free arrangement in grid, center circle, or penalty box
- Each player with a ball, working around cones
- Each player with a ball, moving in a circular fashion around the demonstrator
- Each player with a ball, in pairs facing each other, pretending to take each other on, but when within two yards, using a move to dribble past each other
- Same format, but only one ball, each player taking a turn, and the other acting as semi-passive defender (in this activity go left and right)
- Two lines (no more than three players per line) facing each other ten yards apart, players in front

dribbling towards each other, making a move, passing to player in line facing them, then going to end of opposite line
- Cones in a triangle, up to three players, each with a ball, making a move at each cone (stay at own cone, make move at left cone, then go to right cone)
- Entire team making moves in a grid, slowing down in traffic, speeding up in open space
- Three players in a monkey-in-the-middle configuration, each outside player with a ball dribbling to either side of defender (players must have heads up to read move of other dribbler)
- Three players in a dribble/pass activity using 2 balls
   1. X passes to Y who is in the middle
   2. Y dribbles past passive defender X
   3. X is now in middle and receives from Z
   4. X dribbles past Z to the right side
   5. Z receives from Y at middle area
   6. Z dribbles past Y

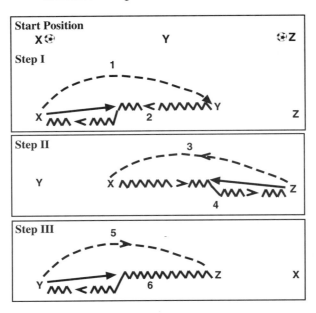

**Diagram #3: Eventually the defender forces the dribbler to go right or left.**

Dribbling the lines of the field can present another variation. Demand moves, backward, turns, changes in speed, some dribbling 'sprints', dribbling lifts, and anything that creates variety and fun.

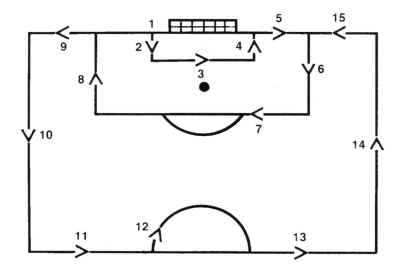

**Diagram #4: Follow the number pattern. This can also be done indoors following the lines of the basketball court.**

Since dribbling is largely a question of personal style, the ball itself is the number one teacher of the player. You can accelerate learning by offering your players a great deal of 1v1 activities. Here is a basic one which has proven successful for all levels, from beginner to highest levels. Use a grid about 10 yards square, three balls, and four players (two per team). Two players go 1v1 in the grid, trying to score by shooting between the feet of the player standing still in the middle of the opposite goal line with feet spread one yard apart. The goal-line players each keep a ball in their hands, so that when the field ball is played over the end line or scored, the goal-line player can immediately toss or roll the ball in to his teammate for a quick counter-attack. Goal-line players can not move except to retrieve the out-of-bounds ball. If the goal-line player is retrieving the ball, his opponent in the grid cannot shoot, but must shield or dribble till the 'goal' returns.

**Diagram #5: 1v1 activities are very rigorous.**

The coach should allow groups to play for a minute or two, then call for a quick switch; the "goals" become the field players for the next minute or two. Demand immediate transition; perhaps use extra players on the side lines to keep the ball in play; require specific moves. Your players will get a great workout as they develop dribbling and shielding skills. Many coaches use some form of this game in every practice, gradually adding players to develop a tactical progression from this 1v1 to 2v1, 3v1, 4v2, and 5v2 (see the next two chapters).

The 1v1 exercise will reinforce the need for shielding. Players will find that when marked tightly and unable to go forward, they must place their bodies between the ball and the opponent, jockeying for position while maintaining possession and looking for an opening. (The concept can be demonstrated by a quick comparison: pick up the ball and dribble it like a basketball; as soon as a defender gets within range, notice how you keep your body between the ball and the opponent.) Coaching points to emphasize are that the body intervenes from a side-on position (adding width to the shield) while balance and vision are maintained. The player must keep cool under pressure, and shielding is working under pressure!

Shielding requires constant movement as you adjust to the defender's position. Playing 1v1 against a superior defender will reinforce this skill, as will 1v1 in a very confined area. To make a game of it, score by counting the seconds of successful shielding. Or add the option of dropping the ball back to your goal-line player after shielding for ten or more seconds.

As much as possible, these activities should involve finishing on goal, because scoring is a skill which requires continuous development and practice. You can progress from the human goal to the flat-faced goals (see "Finishing Activities Using the Two-Sided Soccer Goal" in the appendix) which are very well-suited to many repetitions in a short time. This greatly facilitates economy of training (as well as space, since both sides of the goal can be used safely). Thus you can incorporate the 1v1 with shooting practice.

Need to get your goalies involved? Use full-size portable

goals in a 20x30 yard grid, with two field players going 1v1, and extra balls in each goal for quick restarts. Again, a minute to two at a time, then bring on two fresh field players. Resting players can retrieve balls.

The 1v1 is vital because it is the foundation of the team game of passing and receiving. Once players can execute moves without pressure, it is time to put the moves into more challenging game-like situations. Smallsided games can be used to teach and develop dribbling skills in a more realistic environment. Your players then have the choice of taking on a man, shielding or passing, which is what the real game offers. To encourage dribbling, you can run a smallsided game with specific dribbling demands. For example, players must beat a man before they can pass, or they must touch the ball three times, etc.

All in all, young players must be given time to dribble at practice, and strongly encouraged to practice dribbling on their own. Players can benefit from dribbling instruction. "Individual Attacking" by Shattuck is instructive and entertaining. In practice, give players dribbling experience in many 1v1 and shortsided games. Permit them to dribble in matches, even if they lose the ball! Better to lose the ball attempting to dribble than to kick the ball nowhere. As a developer of young players, encourage the art of dribbling!

First attackers who can dribble cause penetration, open passing lanes, create great difficulty to defenses and score goals.

# 3

# *First and Second Attacker Passing and Receiving Combination Play*

In a very concrete way, dribbling skill is essential to good passing and receiving. Dribbling is a series of micro-passes and collections; without this skill, the player is unable to hold the ball, and is forced to pass it at the wrong time or lose it. Furthermore, the feints used in dribbling can be used to disguise passing intentions. So by developing the individual art of dribbling, the coach is naturally preparing his players for the team art of passing.   Since soccer is a team game, the single most important element in team success is probably the level of passing and receiving. Technically, successful passing requires skillful collection, disguise, proper pace, and accuracy; tactically, it depends on more deception, quality support, creation of space, communication, and variety. In youth coaching, our technical training should concentrate on the basic types of passes and receptions, while our tactical training should teach the concept of support and basic small group tactics. Good training integrates both technique and tactics! The inside-of-the-foot, in passing and receiving, is basic to success in soccer, and is used more than any other technique. Train your players to master it with either foot. At the fundamendal stage, stress the standing foot pointing to the target, the knee bent, the toes raised, the foot striking the ball just above the midpoint and the follow-through. The key to proper weight (pace or speed) of the pass lies in the follow-through, the result of a long stroke. Poor passes are often the result of short, choppy strokes, with no follow-through. The shorter the stroke, the smaller the 'sweet spot'. The sharper timing that this requires is best left to highly skilled players operating at higher speeds. At earlier stages in their lives, they used the longer strokes. With youth, emphasize the follow-through.

At the match-related stage, first add movement, then add token defensive pressure; perhaps a 2v1 in a grid, with the defender playing at 50% effort. Encourage the use of the weaker foot. Notice how the players use their eyes; they should look up before passing or receiving, and look at the ball while passing or receiving. This is important, as it leads to vision and communication. Players can then see the runs made by their teammates as well as their opponents. Hand signals, such as pointing where you want the ball, can also be very effective.

When players are ready for the match condition stage, increase speed and defensive pressure. If you want to keep the 2v1 format, make a game of it by scoring a point for every 8 consecutive passes; keep rotating players between offense and defense every minute or two.

This approach, used to emphasize technique, can be further developed into a 2v2 in a 10x20 yard grid; add small goals and score by passing with the inside-of-the foot through these goals. Building upon this format, you can add players and increase the grid until you have a small-sided game of 5v5 or 6v6. Impose specific demands, especially two touch only, or weak foot only, to develop technique. If players cannot maintain possession, add one or two extra players to one team, or use neutral players who always help the attack.

Since you should try to incorporate shooting into every practice, you may want to add goals (full-size or flat faced) with or without goalies. This approach can be taken with any aspect of passing and receiving. Remember to impose specific demands only for a short time; then allow play without restriction. Encourage movement immediately after passing.

A tried-and-true method for combining technical and tactical work in passing and receiving involves the 1v1 exercise introduced in the previous chapter. After allowing players to take turns going one on one in a grid, give them the option of passing back to their goalies, who must return a one touch pass. This gives them a limited 2v1, as they can only pass backwards. But it will encourage communication and decision-making. The next step is to add a support player on each side; these players are restricted to their respective touch lines and to one touch passes. They support either attacker. Now the give-and-go is a real option. As before, they play all-out for a minute or two, then quickly switch positions.

**Diagram #6: 1-2 move is almost always effective.**

In this drill, the second attackers learn where to support in relation to both the first attacker and the defender; they will soon learn that they cannot 'hide' in the path of the defender, but must move along the touch line to a receiving location. Since they must stay on the touch line, they only have to find the proper space along a single plane.

The next step of the tactical progression advances the second attacker's understanding of support. Use three players in a grid, one in each corner, with one corner open. Passes must follow the lines of the grid; they cannot be diagonal. With each pass, the player with the ball must have support from both sides. Walk them through the following demonstration: Whenever a player has the ball, she must have a supporting player at each near corner. This means that any player in the corner diagonal from the ball must move to the near corner, just as a player on the field might move to support.

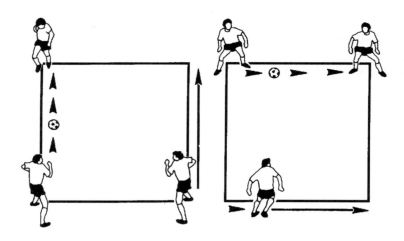

**Diagram #7: Basic support drill is used at all levels.**

Once the players understand where and when to move, increase the speed and limit the number of touches. When they are able to perform this skill with some speed and control for a minute or two, add a defender in the middle of the grid. The first pass is free, then if the defender wins the ball or breaks up the play, he switches positions with the attacker who committed the technical or tactical error. At first the defender can play 50%, slowly increasing his effort to 100%. Get to two-touch, and try for one touch with better players. Show how the outside of the foot pass can disguise the passers intention.

Keep score, such as a point for every string of 10 passes. Merely adjust the size of the grid for appropriate level for any group of players.

Technical/tactical training such as this requires maximum effort for three or four minutes, then a short break. The 3v1 teaches players not only how to pass and receive under pressure, but also how to support the first attacker. The further development of this tactical progression culminates with the third attacker in the next chapter.

As a result of these activities and games, the role of the second attacker will come to many of your players quite naturally. They will discover how to support and make eye contact. Other players may need more instruction, but if you have taught them the roles of the first and second attackers (if not, now would be a good time), they will get the idea of where to move. It is not necessary that they learn the term second attacker, only that they know when and how to support. Support is the first step toward small group tactics, which have the purpose of creating space for the attack.

Train your players to anticipate becoming the second attacker in smallsided games: when a teammate is about to receive the ball, find a supporting position to safely receive that teammate's pass. Often this position is diagonally behind the first attacker. The pass may be to the feet or to space. To emphasize the role of the second attacker, a 3v2 or 4v3 game can be used. Stipulate that first attackers can not penetrate by dribbling or passing until a second attacker offers support. At this stage, for training purposes only, the second attacker could yell "Support!" as he arrives at a good position. This way you can evaluate and correct the player's anticipation and understanding. (During the actual game of soccer, however, offensive communication is largely characterized by vision and runs, whereas defense has much more voice to it.) Once the concept of support is understood, some basic small group tactics can be taught. Introduce the tactic with demonstration and brief explanation, and have players perform it without pressure; try the activities suggested below, then add token pressure, and build up to a shortsided game which demands the proper use of the tactic. As a general rule, it is important to continue to play after executing a pass or movement. Following are the basic two-man tactics that develop the supporting role of the second attacker.

## 1-2 MOVEMENT (WALL OR GIVE-AND-GO)

As shown in the tactical progression, this very basic movement offers support from the side or front of the first attacker: one player passes to another and then accelerates to receive a return pass. One activity to gain abundant trials uses cones and is set up as shown.

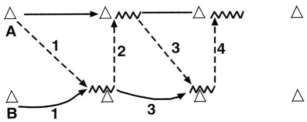

**Diagram #8: Refining 1-2 diagonal passes to develop timing.**

Player A passes diagonally to B, who has accelerated to receive; B dribbles a short distance; players <u>make</u> <u>eye</u> <u>contact</u> and A accelerates to receive a square pass from B; A dribbles a short distance, and the process continues. When going in the opposite direction, the roles are reversed: B passes diagonally and A passes square.

In the next variation, the through pass is emphasized.

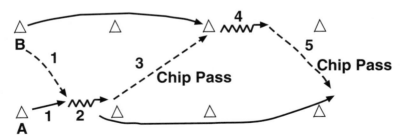

**Diagram #9: Through pass emphasis and technical skill of chipping.**

Player movement is increased and the chip pass is sometimes employed in this more penetrating 1-2 movement.

You can get more players involved in a single 1-2 activity with the following exercise, which highlights the dribbling-passing connection.

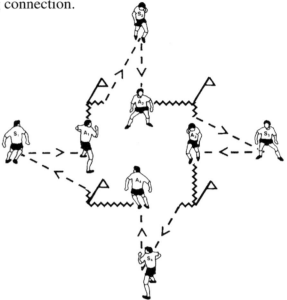

**Diagram #10: Abundant 1-2 move repetition and definitely requires fitness.**

Three to five players dribble around the square, passing to a server at each opportunity. Servers return a square pass to that player. Coach the servers; they are important to the success of this drill. Servers should step toward the ball for receiving, and move back to create space after delivering the square pass. Start with two touch if necessary, but try to get to one touch. Emphasize the first touch, as well as eye contact and acceleration, when coaching passing and receiving.

This activity offers many options. Dribblers can add a hesitation and/or feint before accelerating. They can pass square and servers can return a diagonal pass. Both passes can be diagonal, which increases the pace of the drill. Both passes can be square, forcing servers to move more. Dribblers can add moves to disguise the pass. They can restrict passing to the weak foot or the outside of the foot. (It may help to go in the opposite direction). The square can be enlarged to facilitate accelerating to a drive  (speed dribble).

To develop the drill even further, place the servers inside the square. Or have the dribblers pass to the server one station ahead of them. If your players can do these variations, they are ready for the final challenge: have the servers move along with the dribblers, first in the same direction, then the opposite! In any case, be sure to change roles after two or three minutes. You will easily achieve an abundance of 1-2 moves in a short time, while challenging your players to add appropriate related techniques. All of this develops timing and it is timing that makes the 1-2 movement so effective in beating a defender.

Since the ultimate aim of all passing movements is to finish on goal, you should work toward this in practice. Incorporate the 1-2 movement with shooting opportunities by adding goals. These next two separate activities can be done simultaneously using a single flat-faced goal. Use no more than six players in either activity, so that all players will be moving instead of wasting time in line.

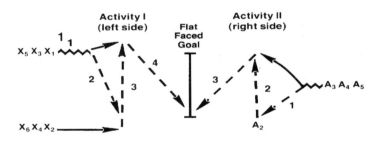

## Diagram #11: Players can never do too much shooting.

On the left side are pairs of players. X1 dribbles a few times, then passes diagonally to X2, who returns a square pass for X1 to shoot. Insist on quality passes and changes in speed. Encourage low shots to the far post. Require players to retrieve their own shots in order to promote the good habit of following one's shot. For added interest require specific dribbling moves, specific passes, or specific shots.

On the right side the player passes to the wall player, who returns a square pass for a shot. The shooter retrieves his ball, then becomes the wall. In this and in many 1-2 drills, coaches often use a stationary player for the wall. While this is acceptable at the fundamental level, the coach should add movement of the wall player at the match-related level. So the wall moves to the ball, and after the touch moves back to create space (stretch the defense). At all costs, coaches must avoid performing the role of the wall themselves; this is something that the players need to learn.

## DOUBLE PASS

Offering support from any direction, a double pass is merely a ball sent from one player to another, and returned with almost no change in position. This sometimes creates time and visibility for penetration. The player with such time and visibility is called a window. From a position behind the ball with a view of the players in front of him, the window can see strikers who are being held at bay by the offsides law. As the window initiates a double pass to a player in front of him, the defense is set in motion. A quick return to the window often opens space for a penetrating pass, such as a first time chip which upsets the defense or even permits a strike on goal.

As this brings a third attacker into play, it will be developed further in the next chapter. At this point, the coach can introduce the double pass as a small group tactic that can be used in combination with others, such as the double pass followed by the 1-2, shown here.

**Diagram #12: Double pass can remove pressure to create time and visibility.**

A10 passes the ball to A6, who immediately returns it to A10; then a 1-2 movement is executed. A6 then runs straight forward initially, so as not to telegraph where he will receive the ball.

Double passes can be used facing the touchlines in order to attain change of field; they are quite effective in throw-ins, and other times can even involve the keeper. At this point it does not make sense to drill extensively with the double pass alone, as it requires no movement, and if emphasized, might undermine the importance of movement in passing. Players with some experience should practice this tactic in combination with others.

However, do point out in shortsided games, where this would be very effective.

## TAKEOVER EXCHANGE

The emphasis on the principle of going to open space in youth soccer makes it important to remember that quality support from the second attacker sometimes requires going to the ball, and even running past the ball and the first attacker. In teaching this principle, the exchange is a very important technique which can raise the tactical mentality of second attackers.

The takeover is not actually a pass, not even a very short one; it is the exchange when a second attacker takes the ball directly from the foot of the first attacker. The takeover can also be faked, so that the ball carrier pretends to leave the ball for his teammate, but at the last instant takes it away himself. This is a great weapon in tight spaces. It exploits the moment when the first attacker has the choice of leaving the ball for a teammate or keeping it for himself, thus confusing the defense.

In takeovers, the first attacker is always in command. To keep the ball, he merely plucks it an instant before the teammate can take it. To give the ball to the teammate, he merely leaves it, while shielding the ball away from the defender. In either case, a sole roll or inside-of-the foot works well for initial contact. Takeovers are done from A1's right foot to A2's right foot, or left foot to left foot. Hand signals are sometimes used in this maneuver; but if the exchange is properly executed, such signals are unnecessary. Practicing this move using left foot to left foot allows for a easy right footed shot, when carried on in the vicinity of the goal.

Takeover runs by teammates to the ball are frequently initiated when a teammate is in such an intense battle to maintain the ball that he cannot raise his head in order to complete a pass.

**Option 1**

Two lines face each other. The dribbling player and receiving player move toward one another and do a takeover.

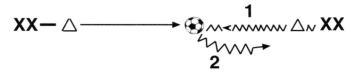

**Diagram #13: Smooth takover requires much repetition to become effective in match condition.**

**Option 2**

Training for the takeover exchange can be facilitated with a circular drill which follows:

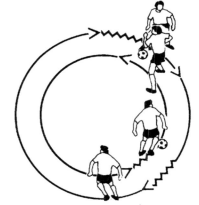

**Diagram #14:**
**Center Circle can be the**
**circle on a soccer field**
**or created with six cones.**

Three to six players dribble counterclockwise inside the circle; a similar number move clockwise outside the circle. When a player with a ball approaches a player without a ball, a takeover move is executed; that is, sometimes the ball is left, sometimes after a complete stop and an indecisive moment, the carrier keeps the ball himself. While the stop is complete, it is just long enough to cause the defender to stop, then there is a rapid acceleration. If both players have a ball, they merely go by one another. Token defenders can be added, and pressure gradually increased. Culminate exchange activities with shooting exercises.

Stress shielding the ball and narrowing the spaces in order to 'pick off' defenders. Do not let defenders slip in between the two attackers without committing a foul. Before the exchange, both players try to see as much as possible in front of them, so as to achieve maximum penetration immediately after the exchange. Steps 3 can greatly disrupt a defense.

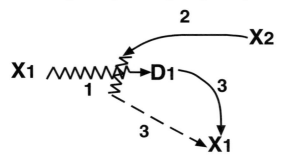

**Diagram #15: After the take over the player without the ball should always consider a penetrating run for a return pass.**

Through the development of the second attacker, we have progressed from individual player techniques and tactics to two man techniques and tactics. For further information, **The Football Association Coaching Book of Soccer Tactics and Skills**, by Charles Hughes, and the accompanying videotapes, are very helpful. Another excellent book on this subject is Alan Maher's **Complete Soccer Handbook.** The Football Association book is excellent for creating space tactics and The Alan Maher book deals with combination play in detail as well as providing dozens of excellent clear activities. A major goal of this training is to combine these tactics with rapidity, variety, and creativity. This so-called 'combination play' advances the game to a higher level; therefore, it is a goal to strive for in the development of better players. The value of such combination play will be clarified in the next chapter, which illustrates the development of the third attacker. This concept will complete the foundation of attacking soccer on the full team level.

Another simple exercise for combination play is sequence passing which merely has 4 players who are numbered 1 through 4. One always passes to two, two to three, three to four and four back to one. Now we merely have one do a 1-2 move with two, and then 3, then 4, and do a takeover with number 2 who also does a 1-2 with each player and a takeover with number three; play merely continues until the cycle has ended. For an added challenge add a defender to the exercise.

Also, all combination play can be completed with groups of three.

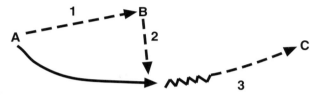

**Diagram 16A: A passes to B and ran for 1-2, then dribbles and passes to C.**

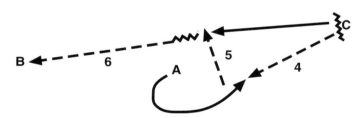

**Diagram 16B: C dribbles in place until A checks away to make a space and then C completes a 1-2 move with A.**

The exercise is a continuous motion exercise that demands serious fitness. It also teaches how to make space for a 1-2 move and is great for timing. Excellent warm-up activity.

Since combination play is the very essence of the beauty of the free flowing game there can never be too much emphasis on it. Two combination plays done in immediate sequence can often destroy the best of defenses.

The ideal culmination of any two man combination is a third man on. A third man on is nothing more than one more pass, usually one touch, which rapidly changes the location (direction) of play.

# 4

# *Creating Space and Development of the Third Attacker*

Another title for this chapter could be "Principles and Methods of Small Group Tactics." These concepts are for players who both understand and implement the roles of first and second attackers. The level of passing and receiving advances with the addition of third attackers, whose primary responsibility is to add mobility. They do this by offering width and depth, which are absolutely essential to the attack. This not only adds to A1's options, but also disturbs the defense.

While a certain amount of A3 development is functional, the basic principles hold true for any position or location on the field. Third attackers attempt to get behind and to spread the defense. When successful, they create the chance for a penetrating pass; when not, at least they draw the defender's attention away from A1 and/or A2, perhaps creating the chance for a penetrating dribble.

The technical aspect of A3 training is a refinement of the basic techniques of passing and receiving. These changes are mainly in terms of time, as A3 often must execute at speed in order to exploit momentary defensive confusion. The tactical aspects involve deciding where, when, and how to run, as well as cooperating and communicating with teammates. These tactical aspects take time, even with professionals! Not surprisingly, the addition of the third attacker(s) challenges the decision-making skills of all players. Thus the training for this role must incorporate a great deal of decision-making activities, rather than predictable drills.

The tactical progression (1v1, 2v1, 3v1) from the previous chapters can be developed into a very good introduction to the role of A3. The next step is 4v2, and takes place in a grid of about 10 yards. Less accomplished players may need more space. Each of the four attackers remains in his respective corner, while the two defenders attempt to win the ball. The object is for the attackers to split the defense with a diagonal pass whenever possible; otherwise they must pass to one of the supporting players at the near corners.

**Diagram #17: A1 was unable to complete the killer pass, but A2 had the opportunity and used it.**

Tactically, this is similar to the real game of soccer in that A1 looks to A2 for support, and to A3 for the penetrating pass. Of course, this 'killer' pass is not always on, and there is defensive pressure, so A1 must weigh the risk of the penetrating pass versus the safety of the support pass. Because the attackers are semi-stationary (only move to be in good location for the through pass), the possession player can more easily look for the penetrating pass.

At the fundamental stage, the coach can walk players through this drill to introduce the concept of the penetrating pass to the third attacker; then increase the defensive pressureand make a game of it by scoring a point for every penetrating pass, or two points for every string of 5-10 passes.

Another option is every penetrating pass counts for two passes. The defender who was in the grid longer switches with the attacker who committed the technical or tactical error. Impose such specific demands as two touch only; award bonus points for the one touch killer pass or good deception. As in the previous stages of this tactical progression, players should go all out for three or four minutes, or until a turnover is made.

This very effective technical/tactical workout will help the coach diagnose the decision-making skills of his players: those who play safely versus those who play risky. This information can become helpful later in deciding player positions; defenders generally need to play for safety, strikers more often need to take risks. But the emphasis here is on good decisions; encourage players to make the through pass whenever it is 'on'.

To further teach the role of the third attacker, a 5v2 exercise is the next logical step in the tactical progression, as it offers more mobility, decision-making, and communication. In a circle of about 15-20 yards in diameter, five attackers keep the ball away from two defenders. The attackers are not limited to the circumference, but they do not enter the very center of the circle, nor overlap each other. As one player moves to receive the ball, the whole circle adjusts to the new situation.

**Diagram #18: 5v2 with movement and the penetrating killer pass.**

As A1 controls the ball, the closest support player moves close to offer support. This leaves the three remaining attackers to offer mobility: one should split the defenders while the others move wide. They need to move quickly and communicate, as the whole circle of players moves with each pass. As in the 4v2, the first pass is free, and the object is to split the defense, which is not always possible. Therefore a strategy develops, as the attackers use the short pass to A2 to draw the defense, then quickly follow with the penetrating pass to A5.

5v2 is often performed with the central midfield playmaker in the middle of the circle constantly changing the ball direction (constantly changing the point of attack). This is then obviously 5+1v2.

Make a game of the 5v2 along the same lines as the 4v2. Since the 5v2 incorporates so much of the passing game, it demands a great deal of coaching. Point out the reason for specific errors in technique or tactics. Many coaches use the 5v2 in every practice, emphasizing movement to support, moving wide or splitting the defense. It is also an excellent device for refining receiving skills: teach players to face the field when receiving a ball without pressure, to use two touch in playing a poorly passed ball, and to use one touch under pressure or when playing a perfectly passed ball. Such decision-making is essential to the development of soccer players and to exciting soccer. The more this exercise stretches the circle, the more it resembles the real passing game. This is a step toward combination play involving three or more players. A three man combination is not simply a string of passes from player 1 to player 2 to player 3; but it more resembles a two man exchange rapidly followed by a penetrating pass to a third player, which surprises the defense. Another example would be a series of wall passes between two attackers, quickly followed by a through pass to a third attacker when the defense is expecting another wall pass. Thus the three man combination passes up the obvious for the more creative, more penetrating movement. A three man combination is characterized by sharp changes in direction, changes in speed, one touch passes, and rapid series of two or more two man combinations.

Ultimately it must be encouraged by creating restrictions requiring it in a shortsided game. This is an absolute necessity because there is now defensive pressure, movement and goal direction. The carry over to the 11 aside is minimal, unless one goes from the exercise to shortsided to the full game.

Another instance would be the double pass followed by the 'window' pass, as introduced in the last chapter.

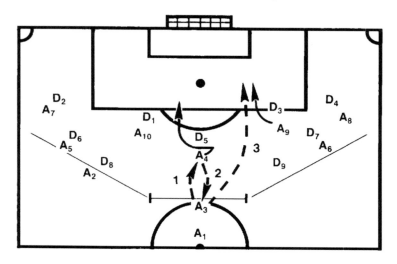

**Diagram #19: Window, through which player views the field in front of him and thus attains much useful information.**

A3 passes to A4, who is under pressure; A4 decides not to turn due to close marking and returns the ball to A3. A3, who has now surveyed the entire front line, chooses the best pass for a forward strike from among several alternatives (in this case a chip to A9).

Of course, shortsided games can be used to develop the third attacker. The objective here is to involve every player, even though only one player can have the ball at any one moment. Players should be taught not to be spectators when a teammate has the ball. The idea is simple: help the attack by running wide or deep. Spreading out is the first principle of attack, and it is best done by the attackers who do not have the ball. Once third attackers see how valuable they are to the attack, they may begin to realize how much fun this role can be.

A useful method in developing the tactical awareness of third attackers is to set up uneven sides, such as 6v4 or 5v3. The larger team exploits its advantage by spreading out, and can easily see the benefits of using third attackers to upset the defense or penetrate. Once the understanding has developed, the sides can be balanced. Now the attackers need to work harder to offer mobility, but their efforts pay off because this is highly match related.

At this stage, the coach can teach specific strategies for third attackers to use in freeing themselves of defenders and creating space. One basic method is the blind-side run, in which the third attacker gets behind the defender so that the defender cannot see both the ball and the third attacker. This creates a moment of confusion that can be exploited by a pass to space, allowing the third attacker to run on to it. In this play, eye contact and acceleration are still important, but this is a situation where pointing hand signals can be very useful. Diagonal runs are particularly effective here.

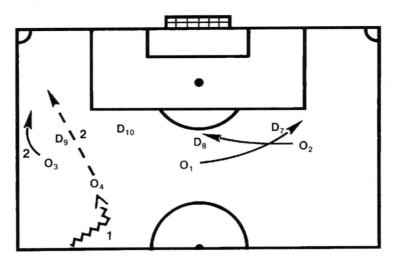

**Diagram #20: O1 and O2 are now really thinking because they are getting themselves open to receive ahead of time**.

O4 (midfielder) delivers ball to O3 who has taken a blind side run on D9. O1 and O2 have both made diagonal runs and may be open to receive a cross from O3.

Another tactic for creating space by the third attacker is the overlap, which exploits the defensive tendency not to mark players behind the ball. This often allows an attacker to make a run from behind the first attacker to a penetrating position. Whether the overlapping player receives a pass or not, the defense must deal with this threat.

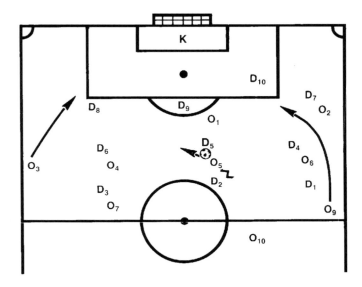

**Diagram #21: Overlaps like 1-2 moves always have a high degree of success even against good defense.**

Overlap: O5 is dribbling toward the goal from a reasonably dangerous location. This must cause the defense to pay attention to O5. O9 takes opportunity to go very far forward causing many difficult defensive decisions. Does the sweeper (D10) mark O9? Does the sweeper focus on the ball, leaving O9 to D7 who already is marking O2? Does the sweeper leave D4 and D7 to take care of O2, O6 and O9 in which case there are 2 defenders covering 3 attackers. Does the marking man to man defense convert to zonal coverage? Generally defenses do not like zones near and inside the 18 yard line.

It seems to be that none of these solutions are very good thus, it is clear to see that overlaps can cause confusion.

In shortsided training, encourage these space-creating tactics. Above all, teach third attackers to spread out the moment possession is gained, and first attackers to look for the penetrating pass. Score a point for each through pass. Instead of traditional end-line goals, place triangular goals on the field. This will encourage third attackers to exploit space and play the ball back to a dangerous area. In a real game, this goal will be replaced by a striker running into this area to receive a pass.

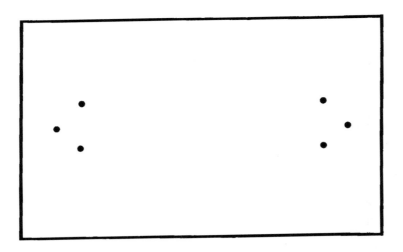

**Diagram #22: The cones or obstacle course markers form a goal which has 3 sides to it.**

Imposing such limitations as two touch or minimal dribbling will encourage players to look for third attackers. Award points for combination play or good decision making. Goalies can get a workout in this game, too; teach them to distribute to the open man running wide.

Other suggestions include smallsided games with four goals - - one at each end, and one at each side.

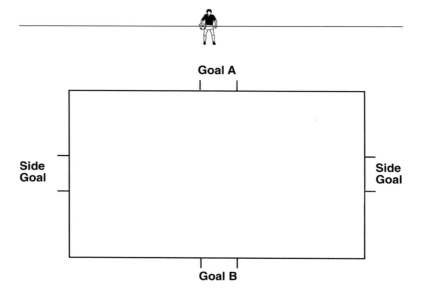

**Goal A**

**Side
Goal**

**Side
Goal**

**Goal B**

**Diagram 23: Either team can score on the side goals. This creates an incentive for attackers to stay wide!**

A variation is to place these goals on the field and allow shots from any direction. At this point the players are involved in a match condition that can include shooting and goalkeeping. Reward third attackers for their anticipating, communicating, decision-making, and space-creating. Let them know that they are helping even when they do not receive a pass.

Once they understand this, they can have fun in the role of the third attacker!

So far we have defined the basic responsibilities of the first, second, and third attacker, and suggested practical exercises and smallsided games that integrate these roles with technique and tactics. This approach to player development is most appropriate for the young American. In countries where street soccer flourishes, such development occurs more or less naturally.

Although some countries that previously had abundant street soccer now find that they too must use these methods to develop players. While the Netherlands leads the way in this regard, England is also very active.

In America (all countries), coaches must create a learning environment where attacking soccer is encouraged, and decision-making by each player is respected. Only then can we incorporate these attacking principles into the full game, refining them according to the location of players on the field. This so called 'functional training' deals with the differences among positions, and should be taught only when the players have a foundation in the techniques, basic roles, and fundamental tactics elucidated in these early chapters. The next chapter clarifies the concepts of functional training by building on this foundation.

# 5

## *Principles of Attack and Functional Training in the Defensive Third*

Understanding the principles of attack can help players create intelligent soccer. These principles can be refined, according to the particular area of the field. For this purpose, the field is often viewed in terms of thirds; that is, the attacking third, the middle third, and the defending third.

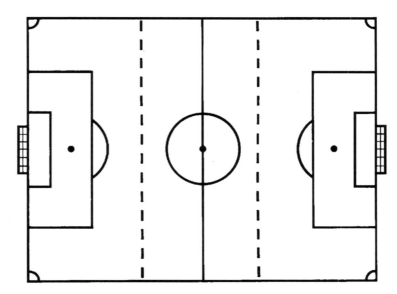

**Diagram #24: The dotted lines show the three 'thirds' of the field.**

On attack, the relationship between maintaining safe possession and taking chances on penetration varies through each third of the field. In the defending third, safety is the greatest concern; players cannot afford to lose the ball here. This is no place to take chances. This is not to say that fullbacks should blindly clear the ball at every opportunity. Dribbling is also permitted, but only if the situation is safe. In the middle third, safety is balanced by a small amount of risk; players may risk more dribbling or penetrating passes when there is a good chance of success. If the ball is lost at midfield, it is not as critical as a ball lost in the defending third, where shots can be taken. In the attacking third, chances must be taken if goals are to be scored! Playing it safe (that is, merely maintaining possession) will not create scoring opportunities. Scoring requires taking risks, with the understanding that possession may be lost. To summarize: in the defending third, play safely; in midfield, balance safety and risk; in the attacking third, take risks.

The principles of attack correspond to the roles of the first, second, and third attackers: penetrate, support, and mobilize. Simply spreading out across the width and depth of the field will help achieve these principles; therefore, players should be trained to spread out as soon as possession is gained. Once the roles of first, second, and third attackers are understood, players will do this automatically, and the coach can then refine their decision-making as to where and how to use the field. Such understanding will ensure that players run intelligently; that is, not everyone will run away from the ball nor toward the ball every time.

This can be accomplished in shortsided training, adding players gradually to reach 11-a-side. At this stage, functional training can begin. Functional training involves adapting the principles of play to a particular third of the field, particular player roles, and considering the safety/risk ratio.

Attack is often begun by a team gaining possession in the defending third of the field. A keeper or defender who mindlessly kicks the ball as far as possible creates a mindless mental set. If the defense develops strategies for mindful possession and forward movement of the ball, a higher level of the game is achieved. The long ball may be used, but there should be an **intended** receiver.

As can be imagined, methods of attack depend to a large extent upon the opponent's style of defense. Therefore, a word about defense is in order here. There are two basic approaches to defense: High pressure and low pressure. High pressure describes a defense that tries to dispossess the offense anywhere on the field. Low pressure refers to a defense that falls back to its own half before applying defensive pressure. Both approaches have their place in the game, and will be discussed in later chapters; what is important at this point is that low pressure defenses drop back to cover some portion of the field in front of their goal. This leaves the attacking team's backs unmarked or with token pressure. Therefore, it is safe to use the backs to begin the attack.

### In the Defensive Third - Using Wingbacks on the Attack

Against a low pressure defense, there is no point in a rapid, risky long ball attack from the defensive third (unless the defense has been caught in transition). Under the normal pace of the game, facing low pressure calls for a full spread of offensive players across the width and depth of the field (full depth means use of approximately 1/2 the length of a field by the field players), and of course a low risk of dispossession. If the goalkeeper has the ball, the wingbacks become the support players. They make bent runs with no thought of stopping until they reach the touch line, or the keeper has released the ball to one of them or to a teammate. Wingbacks must not lose eye contact with their keeper; the bent run ensures vision of the keeper and upfield areas.

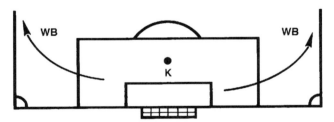

**Diagram #25: Wingbacks need to take very wide fast runs in order to be open. They frequently need to anticipate this action.**

In training, it is often necessary to work with both wingbacks at once, so they get accustomed to making a proper run even when they do not receive the ball. This allows the keeper to deliver the ball to the better run, while also encouraging the keeper to look to both wingbacks.

When the ball is delivered to them, wingbacks always check back to the ball in such a way as to maintain a view up the field. Proper instruction in the 5v2 (Chapter IV) should have enforced this habit of facing the field. The wingback should receive the ball with the foot furthest from the keeper (the foot nearest the touch line). The ball should be closely watched onto the inside of the foot, then directed immediately forward with a single touch. The wingback can then again survey the entire field.

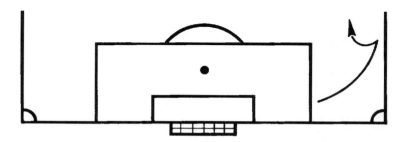

**Diagram #26: Wingback checking back to the ball.**

Target vision is a primary point of instructional emphasis. A player should look at the field before the release of the ball from his teammate, during flight, and immediately after the first touch. Since good keepers feint some throws, the receiver should also be taught to alternately survey the defense and the keeper until the keeper has fully released the ball.

If danger arises, the wingback must be prepared to run back to the ball and return it to the keeper; if the keeper is unavailable, the ball can be cleared upfield or sent out-of-bounds. But frequent blind clearance kicks should be discouraged. Stress good decision-making.

If the wingback can move forward, she should do so immediately. If there is time, the long skip pass to the striker is
considered. This receiver requires support by a midfielder or
some other players.

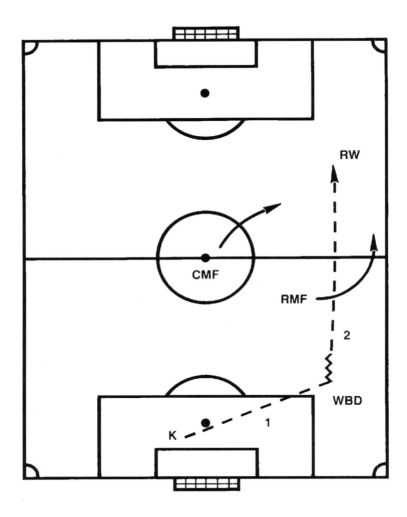

**Diagram #27: The long skip pass.**

This long ball may yield an early strike on goal.

Midfielders must be alerted to the necessity of 'checking out and in', taking runs away from the ball to lure a defender, and then quickly checking back toward the ball to receive a pass. Distant players must go even farther away from the ball so as to deny defenders cover and concentration. Spreading out facilitates much of this, allowing for 1-2 movements, outside and inside overlaps, useful diagonal runs and wingback support of the ball. The diagram below illustrates a 1-2 movement between a wingback and a midfielder.

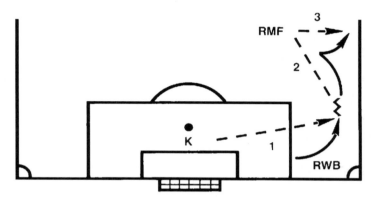

**Diagram #28: Combining with midfielder to move ball upfield.**

Following is a suggested progression for attacking out of the defensive third against low pressure defense. The first step involves two wingbacks, a keeper, and a server. The server takes 20-30 yard shots on goal. The keeper makes the save, then delivers to the wingback who is more open. Repeat until bent runs with good eye contact, quality collection, and upfield vision are well established. When players reach proficiency, add one defender who covers one wingback as soon as the shot is taken. The keeper, of course, delivers to the other wingback. Demand quick, accurate execution.

The next step adds a second defender. One defender marks a wingback tightly; the other defender is 10-15 yards from her wingback. Upon the keeper's release of the pass, the defender challenges for the ball. Ensure the success of the activity by varying the distances, but allow little or no time for the wingback to waste before she delivers a ball back to the shooter. Work at a rapid pace, even to the point of becoming a conditioning activity, but maintain quality as the first consideration.

Adding midfielders to the activity will give the wing backs a target. Then forwards can be included to receive a penetrating 'skip' pass (one which skips the closer player to reach a more distant player). A smallsided game can be the final step: score a point for each good decision by the wingbacks.

This type of activity should last no more than 30 minutes of a practice. It may require two to four practice sessions to complete. The rest of each session must involve many touches of the ball, shortsided work, and game-like decision-making activities which provide more fun, realism, and conditioning.

## In the Defensive Third - Using Centerbacks on the Attack

In a game, the wingbacks and most other players may be marked, which is characteristic of high pressure defense. Since some teams use three strikers, these three players are more likely to mark the 'final four'; that is, the two wing-backs, sweeper, and stopper. This 4+Kv3 situation can be exploited by using the centerbacks (sweeper and stopper) to move the ball through the defensive third. If there are only 2 strikers, many teams will adjust and only commit 3 players to defense.

In a subsequent workout, the above progression can involve two centerbacks instead of (or in addition to) the wingbacks. As before, a server shoots on goal from a distance. Immediately after the server's shot, one centerback moves to one side of the goal outside the penalty area, while the other moves to the opposite side of the goal just outside the penalty area. This lends width and depth to the attack.

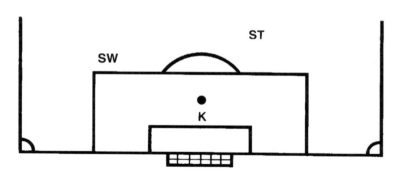

**Diagram #29: This spread generally yields an available receiver.**

A server shoots on goal and immediately covers one of the two centerbacks; the keeper delivers the ball to the unmarked centerback. If players can face upfield, they should certainly do so. But frequently the centerbacks must face the goal or touchline; therefore, voice communication is critical. As soon as the keeper sends the ball to one player, the other back supports and is looking upfield and providing eyes for the ball carrier. Players with such vision should use commands such as

"Turn!"; "Man on!"; "Take it outside!"; "You have support!"; and "Back to the keeper!" Subsequent passes (2, 3 or 4) are suggested in the following diagram. Back to the keeper is less common with the new rule requiring foot passes to keeper be dealt with by feet instead of hands.

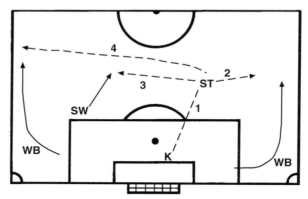

**Diagram #30: The final four make space for each other in this way.**

The essential element is to make it impossible for three opposing strikers to cover four defenders (remembering the keeper makes five) in a full field game. This is accomplished by spreading out across the width and depth of the defending third of the field. Improper positioning allows one opponent to cover two players, as shown below.

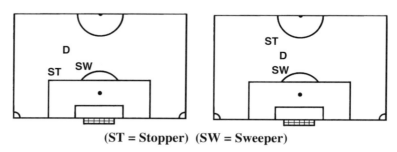

(ST = Stopper) (SW = Sweeper)

**Diagram #31:                    Diagram #32:**
**Both diagrams show poor central defenders positioning.**

The above diagrams show the conventional placement of the free defender (also called sweeper) closest to the goal. In actuality the roles can be interchangeable.

Continuing the progression, a second central defender can be added. This is a very brief situation because it generally precludes a pass to either back, forcing the keeper to send a long ball. Against such a high pressure defense, it is wise to create a rapid strike to beat them long, since the defense may be equal or down in numbers in the finishing third.

The next step adds the two wingbacks so that the final four face two defenders. Emphasize spreading out and proper distribution. In this 4v2, the final four should have no trouble maintaining possession. If so, the coach can add a third defender to create a match-related condition. Stress safety in bringing the ball upfield. Proper spreading is now imperative, especially if the three defenders change to zonal coverage.

To add realism to the situation, the keeper may choose to kick a long ball to an added target player who simulates a 1v1 attack at midfield. This reminds players of the advantages of a 1v1 at midfield or in the offensive third. A 1v1 in the defending third would dictate a long ball by the keeper.

Another option is distribution to a midfield player, particularly an outside one. Infact, this could be the preferred choice because it permits some penetration and the player has defenders as support players.

**Diagram #33: Good hard runs with checking back to the ball gives quick reacting keepers many choices.**

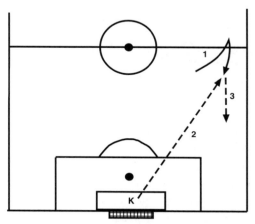

1. Check away and back to ball midfield run
2. A drop kick line drive distribution to midfielder
3. Either a turn, or as shown a layoff to a teammate
The teammate passes forward, diagonally or even a square pass.

This option has been effectively used by accomplished female and male teams as young as 13 years of age.

Like the previous progression involving the wingbacks, this activity can be gradually enlarged to include more players, maintaining the emphasis on safety in moving the ball out of the defensive third. Spending time practicing the entire system against some defense will develop proper runs and communication. Full field scrimmage will reward the initial attack with a strike at goal.

Preparing the final four for attack takes some individualized sessions such as the suggested progressions above. Once the system is learned, a half hour every two or three weeks will help maintain it. Technical weaknesses, such as inaccurate long passes, sloppy collections, and poor dribbling, must be corrected and practiced.

Tactical considerations can begin with the keeper. Sometimes a single failure in moving the ball out safely causes the keeper to kick every ball long, or to overlook one side of the field. In training the final four, look for these common tactical errors: poor runs (not bent) which limit visibility upfield; lazy runs which are too slow to help the attack; fear of using centerbacks even when they are open; and a tendency to possess even when the other team does not withdraw. (This is the time to send the long ball down field.) Tactical problems at midfield often include 'choking' the attack by not moving forward as soon as the keeper has the ball, or not checking back to support when the final four have the ball.

On the team level, the reliance on the blind long ball out of the defending third is a liability. The "If in doubt, kick it out" syndrome should give way to a more positive approach: "I have a good pass that I will execute well." There are times, under extreme pressure, when kicking the ball out of bounds or long is necessary. The guideline for these clearances places the priorities in the following order: "high, long, wide." The blind long kick, however, usually reaches the opponent. Often times, if there is enough time and space for a long delivery, there is probably enough time and space to do something constructive with the ball. High level soccer is characterized by quality passes, and even the long clearances have an intended receiver. In any case, there are great rewards for teams that learn patience and possession in moving the ball out of their final third. Such play sets a tone of teamwork, confidence, and patient development of offense by allowing every player to dribble, possess, and combine. Furthermore, it allows defenders to strike and score. Above all, it encourages all players to think. And it is only with thinking that high level soccer can be attained!

Nothing is more beautiful than the total soccer player, playing on a team that uses both short and long passes and balances possession with penetration. Varied rhythms causes lack of easy prediction by the defense and greatly enhances scoring. Not surprisingly, no one does it better than World Cup Champions, Brazil.

# 6

## *Functional Training in Midfield*

The mere mention of midfield launches many soccer coaches into heated argument. But it is important to remember that the great midfield debate takes place off the field, and concerns professional teams. Youth coaches need not be unduly influenced by such theoretical discussion as the merits of the Dutch system versus the Italian. This chapter focuses on the development of intelligent midfield play in accordance to what the defense does. While the approach is a systematic one, it encourages decision-making, and actually fosters creativity.

As in the final third, the principle of spreading out still holds true at midfield. Remember that we are dealing with an area on the field, not a position *per se*. Just as play in the defensive third is not restricted to the defenders, midfield play is not restricted to midfielders; all field players often find themselves as linkmen for strikers and defenders and must play the game accordingly. In other words, they must balance safety and risk, get support, try to penetrate. With numbers up or even, attack quickly and directly; with numbers down, build up slowly and work for an opening. Some back passes may be necessary in order to balance risk and safety.

At midfield, the roles of first, second, and third attacker still come into play; but now there is the addition of rear support for safety. As in the final third, the midfield attack usually takes what a defense gives. Thus the choices of getting the ball through midfield vary according to the defense's tactics. On occasion, it is good to impose your own style to test and surprise the defense.

But here the instructional emphasis covers the various choices at midfield, based on what the defense does.

In any third of the field, the attack generally needs at least four players in that area. It is nearly impossible to have proper ball support and some mobility without four or more players in the third of the field where the ball is. With a three man midfield line, four man width across the midfield is generally created by one of the final four moving into the middle third. Of course, the four man width at midfield can be provided by any of the four defenders, with all midfielders and strikers in the attacking third. (This would happen against very low pressure.)

Whether the ball is delivered to midfield by the keeper, a defender, or a midfielder, front runners move up to create forward depth, some defenders stay behind the ball to give depth from the rear. Now the midfield offers width and intelligent choices to the first attacker. Let us look at those choices, beginning with a midfield attack against a high pressure defense.

Since high pressure defenses cover players all over the field, attacking forwards often have only one defender between them and the goal. Therefore, the first option would be a **long ball** to the wing or even the center forward drifting out toward the touchline. This tactic requires multiple rear support from midfielders. The advantage of this direct attack lies in getting behind several defenders with one pass, and in the tendency of the defenders to allow open lanes on the wing. It is very effective when it connects with a player who is strong in collecting (esp. air balls) and distributing or shooting in traffic.

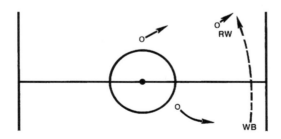

**Diagram #34: Long ball wing strike. In the modern game 5 or 6 midfielders is not uncommon.**

This can be 'over-the-top' ball forward, or more commonly the striker checks back to the ball.

A second option against high pressure would be a **1-2 movement** with a midfielder who is checking back. This would beat a single defender who is pressuring the ball, and does not require the long distance accuracy of the first option. Other two-man tactics (double pass, take over exchange, and overlap) can also work here, as high pressure defense may be susceptible to a 2v1 attack. Here the 1-2 involves a wingback and the center midfielder.

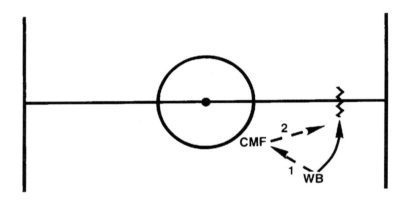

**Diagram #35: A 1-2 movement. This play sometimes utilizes up to 30 yards - - in any case the distance varies considerably from one occasion to another.**

The third option is a long **diagonal pass**. This change of field often catches a defense moving the wrong way, thus opening a channel of attack. Like the first option, a long penetrating pass takes several defenders out of the play. Strikers may then be able to get free for a shot on goal.

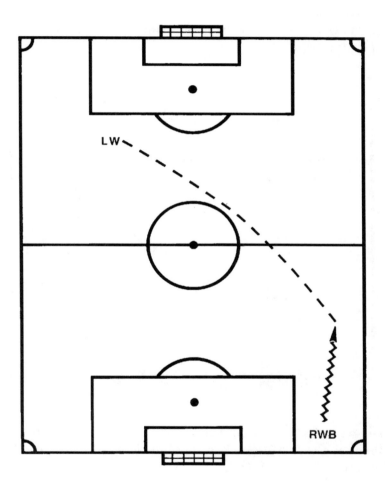

**Diagram #36: The finish can be direct, or a layoff, cross or combination play can precede the shot.**

Against low pressure defenses, the use of wingbacks as explained in the previous chapter can advance the ball through midfield. **Combinations** involving the centerbacks and-or marking backs are also effective. This option shows a slower and more patient movement of the ball. The keeper distributes to the wingback, who combines with a centerback. The diagram shows a 1-2 movement, but a takeover exchange or an overlap could also be used in the event of sudden defensive pressure.

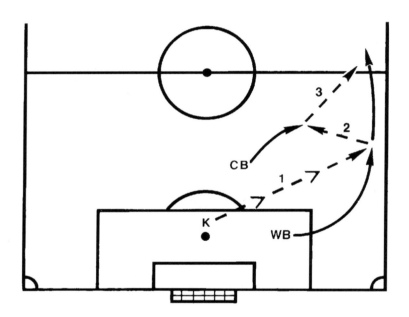

**Diagram #37: Building attack from defending third and through the midfield. All of these movements could also be performed by midfielders or any combination of players.**

Another option is a long dribble through the midfield by one of the final four. This can surprise a low pressure defense which retreats too slowly, or a high pressure defense which leaves a back unmarked.

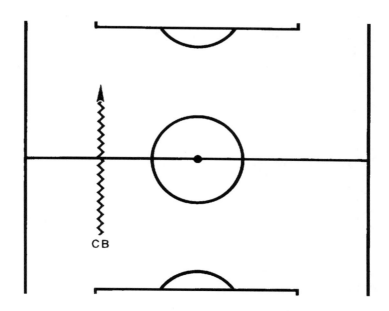

CB

**Diagram #38: Dribbling attack. With more total soccer players available than ever, high level play has become more characterized by defenders who dribble when safety permits. This is frequently done by midfielders.**

In developing good decision-making and skill at midfield, the following progression is suggested. As always, the coach can adapt these activities depending on the players' needs. The first step uses short passes in developing possession and exploitation of the midfield area. Four players use the entire width of the field while passing the ball from **touchline to touchline**, then back again. After every pass the two outside players must touch the touchline. Emphasize upfield vision, crisp passes, movement toward the ball, and efficient collection throughout the circuit. Involve the entire team in this progression as width is a necessary concept for all players.

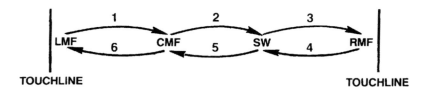

**Diagram #39: Midfield width permitting changes in point of attack.**

After each pass, the player must move away and be prepared for a return pass. Emphasize the importance of each player moving toward the ball to receive it.

The next step uses the same format to introduce the skip pass. On the first circuit, the first pass is to the closest player, and the second pass is a 'skip pass'. Every other pass is a skip pass until the ball returns to the first player. This time the first player begins with a skip pass and the other players alternate accordingly.

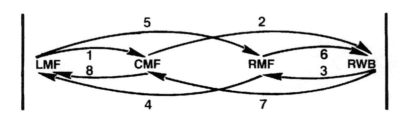

**Diagram #40: Rapid change in point of attack as result of long ball usage.**

When players grasps the concept, add forward movement through the midfield. For all ages, emphasize accuracy. Better players should use air balls for the skip pass, and can try proper bending of the ball and even takeover exchanges.

As players become proficient in the skip pass, add other tactics for forward movement: the wall pass, the double pass combined with a skip pass, a diagonal pass followed by a square pass, and a square pass followed by a forward pass. The last two diagramed below.

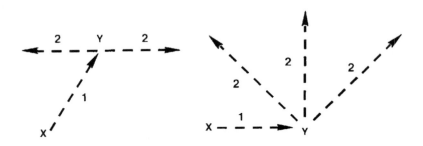

**Diagram #41:**
**Forward pass followed by a square pass.**

**Diagram #42:**
**Square pass followed by diagonal or straight forward pass.**

The next step adds a striker who shoots on goal. After one or two changes of field, midfielders deliver a ball to the striker. For the first several tries, the striker will shoot. Then the striker can alternate shooting with laying the ball off for a midfielder to shoot. Encourage the use of all combinations, and allow everyone repeated shooting opportunities.

To advance to a match-related activity, set up a scrimmage of 11 attackers versus 6 defenders and a keeper on a full field. The team of eleven should possess the ball and change fields in each third, finishing with a shot on goal. (They may need a dry run without any opposition.) Obviously, no team should ever be so stretched out, but this will allow good practice in changing fields and developing width. The team of six is divided into three pairs. Each pair must remain in a particular third of the field while defending against the attacking team.

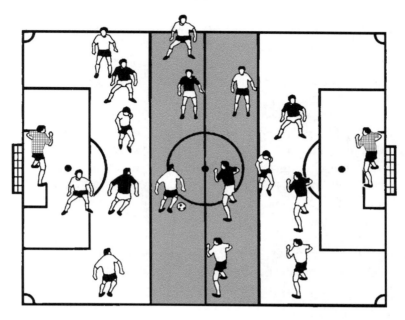

**Diagram #43: Team must remain spread out, but still go toward every pass. This is a great activity - - try it and after one or two occasions incorporate your own wrinkles!**

In this situation, **insist upon four man width wherever the ball is**. One of the final four must join the midfield, two of the midfielders must join the forwards when the ball is in the final third. The final strike is made by a cross with all three slots (near post, far post, and penalty area) filled. This progression can work up to the match condition by building up to 11v11. Reward every change of field, and use low pressure defense. When the attacking team is repeatedly successful, change the defending team to high pressure. Now the attack must be more direct. Look for a change in attacking tactics; the offensive change in behavior must come from the players. Once it does, the coach can secretly signal to the defense to change back and forth from low to high pressure. The offense must learn to react properly on its own, using both direct play and deliberate build-up. At this stage, midfield play will approach a higher level of soccer. Players will observe a defensive change and learn to adapt to it. They will seek to exploit change and learn to adapt to it.  They will seek to exploit space wherever the defense allows; at a more advanced level, some players may even create chances where none appear to exist.

This adaptation to the defense and exploitation of space are the objectives in teaching systematic forward movement. Despite some claims to the contrary, a systematic attack actually encourages greater creativity. The mere elimination of confusion fosters the imagination, and the four man width allows choice. Teaching systematic tactics demands a special effort on the part of the coach; but all this planning, choosing, and practicing will allow the attack to take place without all concern being focused on merely maintaining possession.

Once players do not just knock the ball into the final third, nor forget where the goal is, the proper mental framework is partially understood.  Once they realize that the midfield is an area in which we **PROBE** to put the ball into the box with reasonable control, midfield play is fully understood.  These exercises not only teach the proper techniques and tactics, but they also inculcate the proper psychology of midfield probing.  The initial premise that players must clearly understand the basic roles of first, second, and third attackers now holds true more than ever. These basics must be achieved before teams can succeed in the tactics and functions that make versatile midfield play a major part of exciting soccer.

# 7

# *The Strike and Functional Training in the Attacking Third*

All too frequently, players and teams are criticized for weaknesses in attacking, yet more often than not, these youngsters receive little or ineffective instruction about attack. The mere mention of attack is a long way from developing the skills for attractive attacking soccer. Of course, spending a great deal of time on the tactics clarified in this chapter, without accompanying technical instruction and practice, is not enough. But when combined with psychological, technical and tactical instruction, this chapter offers proven methods for increasing the frequency and quality of the greatest moments in soccer -- the scoring of goals!

In the attacking third of the field, the safety/risk ratio emphasizes risk; that is, taking chances in order to put the ball into the net. This requires an understanding that possession is often lost in the attacking third. Against a good defense, merely maintaining possession is not enough to create scoring opportunities. A team must be willing to risk losing the ball, though not to the point of recklessness.

Finishing activities are seriously lacking both in the U.S. and throughout the world. The typical player pre game or pre training approach frequently involves players taking direct kicks from inside the penalty box, which never happens in a game! Another method is the use of shooting drills, but drills alone do not make good finishers. The best way to develop goal-scorers, while they are becoming technically efficient, involves real game situations: working up to full speed against two or more defenders in a tight area. The importance of this approach can be seen in the fact that all previous chapters prescribe activities which culminate in realistic striking at goal opportunities.

Again, shortsided games using full-size goals and goalkeepers in a small area afford numerous shots on goal. If players have learned the correct shooting technique, and followed the progressions suggested in this book, they already have had much more shooting practice than most teams. They can then begin to develop the mental toughness that goal-scoring requires.

Goal-scoring is an attitude. Shooting is merely kicking the ball toward the goal, while finishing is putting the ball into the net. Therefore, players should be taught to think in terms of finishing, not just shooting. This is not simply a matter of semantics; instead, it deals with the development of a positive attitude and the proper mental framework. The biggest mistake in the attacking third is a mental one -- failure to shoot!

Another critical mental factor is timing. In today's game, there is no longer the luxury to stop, look, and play. Nor can players run to space only to stand and wait for the ball; they must arrive as the ball arrives. All players must be alert to the timing of a run. With a full speed run there is a chance to get open at an ideal location. Since there is always the possibility of a quality defense or slight technical difficulty by the striking team, attackers must also be instilled with the habit of second effort and follow-up on each striking attempt.

Of equal importance is the realization of when to shoot. Many players think that they have to get fully behind the defender before they can shoot. In fact, all they need is a 'window', just enough space to get a shot past the defender and on target. Thus they can benefit from the encouragement to shoot early, as soon as a window or reasonable chance to score presents itself. Keeper errors, visual screening, rebounds, deflections, and just plain luck all increase the chances of scoring, but only when shots are taken, and mostly when they are taken early, but in accordance with what **is** available. The mental preparation and decision-making in the attacking third are based on the principles of player roles and of attack. But these principles are slightly adapted because of the space limitations in this part of the field: deep in the attacking third, teams must often penetrate across the field, and the classic triangular formation of first, second, and third attackers often become compressed. Forward penetration gives way to getting the ball to scoring location.

The previous chapter points out that there is nothing automatic or stifling about systematized midfield play, and this fact holds true in the attacking third as well. It is vital that players know what to do in the attacking third; that is, to make good decisions from knowledge which avoids panic. Therefore, we will examine the choices available to the first attacker in the finishing third of the field.

The first option will begin near the touch line entering the final third. The wing (or player in the wing's role) will drive toward goal, and if he beats the defense and has a reasonable shooting angle, will take a direct shot on goal. The first option for any attacker in the penalty area with half a chance should be to finish! This may seem obvious, but players often neglect this option. Only realistic practice will perfect the techniques and set the proper mental framework.

It is well researched that most goals are scored from close in - - 10 yards or less. None-the-less the mental set of taking available opportunity is a must. Obviously, if a player is marked and a teammate is wide open the pass must be given. What must not happen is a player in 1v1 situation passing to another player who is in a 1v1 situation.

The use of 1v1 contests which culminate in a strike are excellent preparation, as are 1 v 1 v 1 v K and 1v3+K in the penalty area, illustrated below. If necessary, have defenders offer token pressure or be 'crab' defenders. Also players can be placed along the sides for 1-2 movements to ensure success of the activity. The attacker (A) beats D1 with a dribble, then tries to beat D2 and finish on goal. Defenders are confined to their individual grids, and the keeper may not leave the goal area until the last defender is beaten. Set up several stations, each with groups of four to eight players. Move to full pressure and keep score to encourage maximum effort. Rotate defenders. Since this activity focuses on the attack, avoid coaching the defenders. Good instruction avoids confusion by working with one element at a time, and teaching that element well.

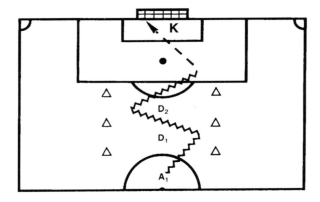

**Diagram #44: 1 v 1 v 1 v K  Developing attacking confidence. It also puts a player in an exercise in which he continuously moves TOWARD the goal.**

Since attackers often find themselves marked by two or more defenders, they must learn to deal with this situation in practice. A 1v3 + K activity offers such a challenge, and also helps an attacker to feel relatively 'free' in a match when he/she has a 1v1 or 1v2 opportunity. Allow the attacker to receive the ball from the servers before the defenders become active. Gifted players will find ways for defenders to interfere with each other.

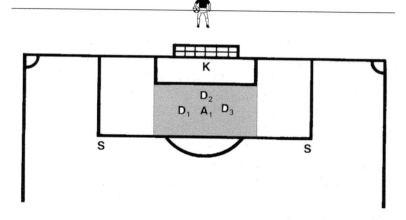

**Diagram #45: 1 v 3 + K Attacking confidence; move servers to create many varied situations. Ground, driven, bouncing, slow rollers are all wonderful possibilities.**

On any trial, each server has a ball, and either may serve. At early stages, 50% pressure or weak defenders may be used, but work up to attacking success against full pressure. The rewards of this activity are great and well worth the effort. In some cases, the two servers may receive a pass when A1 is under pressure, but they must return the ball one touch to A1; servers cannot move or shoot.

Another option is merely 4 players with every player taking on the others. In this situation a coach serves the ball, attempting to give opportunities for all four players. Serve ground, driven, air and even bouncing balls throughout the entire shaded area. This is an exhausting activity: therefore change personnel or provide rest.

In these activities, as in a real game, the attacker is generally advised to shoot for the far post. The goalkeeper usually concentrates on the near post more than the far post. At first you might want to restrict the keeper to the near post. Also there is a better chance for other attackers at the far post, especially on a rebound or keeper deflection. Later, chips or near post shots should be taken when they are the best choice. Again, players must be allowed to make decisions in the workout if they are to develop decision-making ability during games.

Another suggested activity that encourages finishing and decision-making involves a pair of flat-faced goals. A neutral server delivers the ball to one player, who attempts to beat the other with a shot on goal. The server can begin by alternating serves, then repeating serves to the player who scored last, and finally offering neutral serves for which the players must compete. More players can be added, or the server can become a second defender. Another variation is to serve air balls, and limit scoring to head balls. For advanced players, the corners of the goals can be highlighted with tape to offer a more precise target. The versatility of these goals allows for other 1v1 activities on the outer faces of the goals.

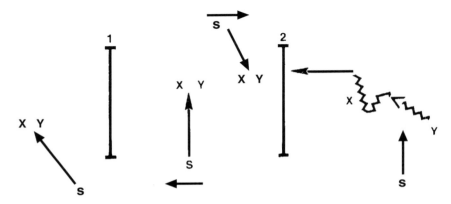

**Diagram #46: 1 vs 1 Shooting on first opportunity. These 2 goals are accommodating 8 players - - 4 'keepers' could also be added.**

Of course, reasonable shooting chances do not occur every time a striker enters the attacking third. The second option, therefore, is to cross the ball. The player usually tries to gain as much ground toward the goal as possible before crossing, since this creates the most dangerous chances on goal. Receivers can then face the goal for a powerful first-time shot. The problem of off-sides is also eliminated when the server penetrates to the goal line.

The preferred dribble or drive aims for the end line, attempting to stay within twelve to fifteen yards from the goal, as shown in diagram #47. A drive to the goal line as shown by A, as opposed to B, is greatly preferred.

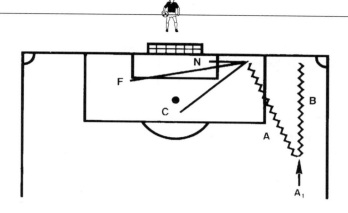

**Diagram #47: Giving the receiver good shooting angles.**

There are three target areas for the cross: far post (F), near post (N), and center (C). Ideally, all three areas would become occupied by attackers just as the ball is about to arrive.

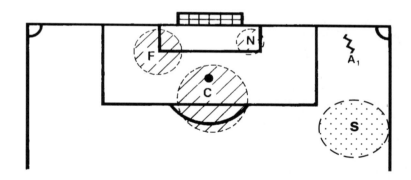

**Diagram #48: F, N, and C lined areas are the target areas for all serves.**

If the defender forces a blind cross, in other words plays well enough to keep the winger's head down, the cross should be a lofted ball to the far post, over the keeper's head and out from the goal line. The receiver can then face the ball and the goal without an awaiting keeper. For this cross, emphasize the non-kicking foot pointed toward the target. If the wing can make eye contact with a teammate at the near post, the cross is generally a low driven instep kick that the receiver can deflect toward the goal with the head, or flick on to a third attacker. This requires timing and heading skill, which are the result of much practice. Higher level soccer is characterized by such technical and tactical capabilities as the flick-on. Noteworthy are the 1986 World Cup Final, where West Germany used the flick-on for both goals, and the 1987 NCAA Finals, where Clemson won with the same play.

A third choice is a lofted, driven, or ground ball to the central area. In any case, a 'friendly' one touch ball is preferred. This play depends upon the keeper's position, defenders' and attackers' location, as well as skill and field conditions.

Frequently the best a server can do is to serve the ball between the defense. If the entire team is trained in this regard, all runners attempt to fill lanes between defenders. This provides a far greater connection between server & receiver, and can result in many goals.

The words wing, striker, attacker etc., are used somewhat interchangeably. This attack can be used with any formation, system of play and with teams composed of very differing attacking talents.

Crosses are only as effective as the receiver's heading skill. Players need to master two types, the attacking header and the clearing header. Both types are useful to all players because strikers must clear balls, as in defending against corners, and defenders must pass air balls to the feet of their teammates and also shoot. The emphasis of the attacking header is on getting the ball down. The ball should bounce perpendicular to the keeper's feet, usually close to the goal line. Contact is made with the frontal area of the forehead (the flat part). For the clearing header, contact is made higher on the forehead (more on the hairline). Stress distance and height.

Attackers must specifically practice the scoring header, since it requires both concentration and confidence. Without practice, all techniques deteriorate, but those that demand courage need additional work.

In lieu of a cross, the wing may pass a perfectly weighted ground ball to a supporting attacker (S, in dotted area) for a one touch shot, cross, or series of dribbles to the goal line for a cross.

Often young players cannot loft a ball to the far post or drive a ball accurately to the near post; therefore, the emphasis should fall on the pass to the central area and to the supporting attacker. At higher levels all four options should be fully developed, though individual skill, team style, and opponents ability may determine the emphasis.

Since a great number of goals are scored from the area between F, N, and C, why not put attackers there? The answer is that this area must remain **vacated** so that it can be **exploited** by anyone of three people coming into areas F, N, and C at speed.

Functional training for the cross can teach your players their individual responsibilities. Let's focus on who might try to strike at each area. A coach must be open minded to variations best suited to his unique personnel. While the basic system is sound, the coach can adapt variations, depending on the players' skill and attitude. Sensible adjustment and emphasis of a basic system might be wiser than trying to invent a whole new system. Minor changes allow for many options, which the youth coach needs to adjust due to variance in team skill, individual player strengths and personnel available from game to game.

Generally, the center forward would go to the far post area in order to blindside the central defenders. Since the center forward is usually marked by a good defender, it is advantageous to remove this defender from the vital near post area. Area F presents opportunities to score with the head, and center forwards are most often willing and able to head the ball from this vital location. Other players could occupy the F location; the left wingback or left midfielder are logical candidates, especially if they can head the ball well.

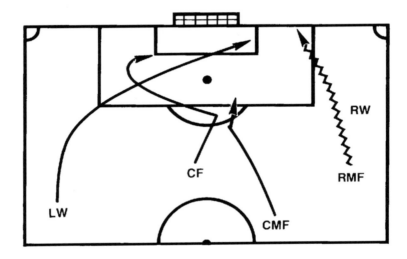

**Diagram #49: Filling the 'spots' in attack.**

The near post location is frequently attacked by the left wing attacker (diagram #50). This requires a lengthy run across the field, which can upset the defense. Forcing the defender to change sides of the goal, or to pass his marking responsibility to someone else can cause confusion. The attacker may also be able to outrun the defender to arrive at the near post unmarked.

If the crosser is deep, path 1 is the first option; if the crosser is not deep, path 2 can be taken to maintain an on-sides position. A disguised and quick movement along path 3 can then exploit the near post area. Maintaining on-sides is fairly simple for the left wing because she can see the ball and the deep defenders throughout the approach.

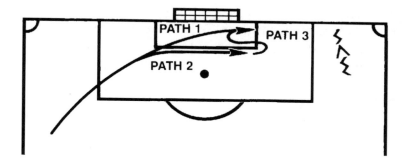

**Diagram #50: Wing run with full visibility for maintaining an on-sides position.**

Of course, the wing attacker can receive anytime after entering the box, and then take a shot. On the other hand, if the wing does not receive the ball early, he should continue toward the first attacker to offer support. The point is not to remain stationary. **Successful strikes at goal are characterized by timely movement.**

Area C is often assumed by the center midfielder, who is often chosen because of the ability to offer quality support to teammates. In this case, however, an attempt at early support may well deny a shot on goal. Because this is an easy area to get to early, the major problem with this location is early occupancy. Patience must be emphasized, so that the midfielder will learn to arrive at the last possible moment, running at speed. Teach the basic movements first, and only then coach timing.

Along with the timing of this run, all involved players must be taught what to do if the ball arrival is delayed: all three players merely rotate clockwise with right wing attacks, counterclockwise with left wing attacks. This allows visual contact with the ball and movement, while forcing decisions among defenders. Any breakdown may result in a goal. After players have practiced this attack, it merely becomes a general pattern in which creativity is encouraged. But, during the training period, maintain discipline. Variations are permitted only after the general pattern is established. Once the artist knows the media, he can become fully creative.

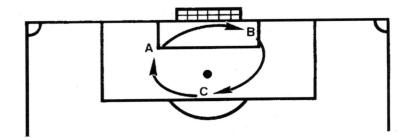

**Diagram #51: Movement for delayed crosses**

The run to area S (diagram #52) is generally made by the right midfielder, although it could be the right wingback, stopper, or sweeper. In any case, this player is the second attacker, and as such must concentrate on the role of supporting the first attacker. Any player who goes directly to area S is likely to be marked. Therefore, he must be in the general area, but still able to make a run to a desirable location to receive the ball. Changes of direction and speed facilitate the support function.

This could be accomplished in many ways, but the key is to provide support through bent run movements while the wing attacker works for a quality pass. A run as shown in the diagram below may blind side the defender; then a cut can be made in front for a one touch shot, or a bent run back to receive a chip over the defender's head. In any case we want this player to attempt to get free for a shot on goal or pass to a teammate.

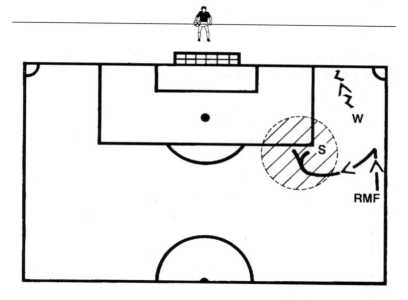

**Diagram #52: All players near ball should be working hard to attain a shot on goal.**

Once a team has mastered the basics of filling the critical attacking areas, the particular locations N, F, C and S can be filled by anyone. When such a free lance occupation takes place, the general order is as follows: the first player who can get to the near post does so, the second player takes the far post, the third player fills the middle. This order permits all players to use their vision effectively; no one needs to look backwards, which is difficult and time consuming.

Here is an **effective activity** for teaching your players to fill the attacking slots. Groups of four players stand inside the midfield circle.

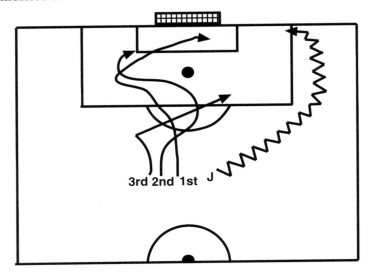

3rd 2nd 1st

**Diagram #53: Filling attacking slots integrating fast thinking. Later on it will be a habit; it will merely be a reaction which is faster, therefore more efficient.**

Ground balls to behind the penalty spot are emphasized. One player is given the ball and dribbles to the goal line inside the penalty area. Service is to all 3 locations, but the area just behind the penalty spot is emphasized. Then the first runner to the near post goes wide outside the far post six yard box timing his run at the near post for when the dribbler delivers service. The coach either holding shirt (or verbally) releases the second runner to far post who is also wide. Then the third runner for the penalty area is released. THE MAJOR FOCUS IS PROPER LOCATION RUNS AND TIMING.

Then add a single defender and keeper. The single defender marks one runner; changing who he marks on each occasion. The server MUST serve to one of the two open runners. I found this exercise remarkably valuable in creating scoring opportunities and actual goals. In time 2 or 3 groups can do the activity at the same time, either with assistant coaches,

captains or the head coach monitoring all groups simultaneously. Again a flat faced goal could accommodate two
groups.  Generally the whole team is trained, but obviously
strikers are engaged in this activity more often and for greater
periods of time.

Simply move from this stage to a shortsided game (anything
from 5 v 5 to 8 v 8 is appropriate), still using full sized goals.
Goals scored from a goal line cross count 3 points while
direct dribbling goals count 1 point.  Be certain players fill
the slots, approach the goal from angles taught and that players do not arrive too early.

Though this training does not exhaust the possibilities of
wing attack, it does teach players the major options, thus mit-
igating confusion. It will also encourage players to attack on
the wing, making better use of the entire field. This approach
is highly recommended before attempting to develop direct
attacks up the center of the field. These more direct attacks
are characteristic of higher level teams that are already capable of wing attack. On the youth level, direct attack often
deteriorates to kick-and-run, poor decision-making, lack of
patience and improvisation, as well as, impoverished technical development.  Nevertheless, direct strikes are a part of the
game, requiring intelligent training that should minimize its
negative aspects at younger levels. But this training should
occur only after the fundamentals of wing attack have been
mastered. Since reasonably developed defenses seldom allow
a through ball at the goal, direct attacks require someone to
turn the ball at the goal or quality combinations creating a
shot. Players need to practice this difficult skill so that they
can prepare the ball with one touch, turn quickly, then shoot
accurately and powerfully with the second touch. Ability to
turn both left and right in a variety of ways is a great asset.

Using this drill, train players to receive ground balls to either
foot, and air balls to the foot, thigh, chest, and head. Then add
disguise: on a turn call, feint a touch, let ball through legs and
then pass it. Another feint involves the inside of one foot to
one touch the ball behind the other foot, setting up a pass or
shot. As might be expected, this activity should culminate
with finishing on goal and keeper.

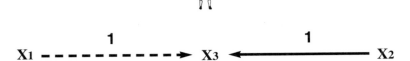

$$\overset{\textbf{1}}{X_1} ----- ---\blacktriangleright \quad X_3 \blacktriangleleft \overset{\textbf{1}}{\rule{3cm}{0.4pt}} X_2$$

**Diagram #54: X1 would tell X3 "Man On." Man on would indicate a return pass to X1; in any case X3 would not turn.**

To develop this skill arrange three players in a line. Player X1 passes to player X3; player X2 becomes a defender. The passing player must make the proper call: "Man on!" if the defender marks closely, "Turn!" if the defender gives space. After turning player X3 can pass to player X2 and the drill continues. Player X3 remains in the middle. Rotate players every 3 minutes. If player X3 cannot turn, he must shield, then move toward player X1 to create space to turn, dribble, or simply pass the ball back to X1.

Shortsided work for the day should score a point for every successful call of "Turn!" or "Man On!" For every mistaken call, deduct a point. Let teams keep their own score and call it out. The thinking while playing is a feature of the real game. Soccer requires a great deal of thinking about several things at once. Sometimes we're measuring our opponents speed, style, etc., yet we are playing to score (soccer is almost never played the same way when we are winning as opposed to losing). In addition, we may be trying to conserve energy but not give up too much. All this is done while still playing, reacting to support, warding off a tackle, penetrating, etc. Much of this is reaction, but some of it is conscious thought.

Accomplishing all that is outlined here is likely to be a long range plan of at least two seasons for a team which meets twice a week during the season. However, this is no reason to avoid training for a quality attack. Once players have learned one systematic attack, they will have an easier time learning others. Certain formations lend themselves better to certain types of attack. Systems using traditional wings obviously suit themselves to the wing attack system advocated here, whereas a double striker formation offers target players for direct attack. But the choice of formations depends most directly on the individual players' abilities and weaknesses.

None-the-less, in either attack players should understand how to fill the slots.

Some motions that are part of a more direct attack are often characterized by a 4-4-2 formation. First and foremost the two strikers does not mean the team strikes with 2 players. It only means that there are two DESIGNATED strikers. We still need 2 or 3 others to join in the attack in order to score goals.

The two designated strikers must work together - - often in tandem, one in front of the other, but not usually flat across the field. In this way they can work TOGETHER because obviously two lone strikers working alone are not going to score many goals. However, on defense the two strikers might be flat. Furthermore, both strikers are usually on the strong (ball) side of the field.

If one can hold the ball to allow midfielder or wingbacks to get forward, this will help enormously.

What follows is a number of options, but generally any given team would probably emphasize 2 or 3 options best suited to the talents of that particular team.

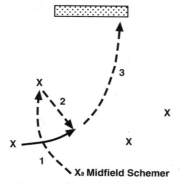

**Diagram 55: Layoff**
This is a simple delivery to a target player, then a layoff for the other striker for a shot on goal.

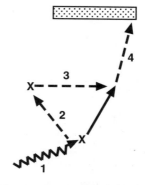

**Diagram 56: 1-2 move**
Another simple option is a 1-2 move by the 2 strikers or ANY two players, though frequently at least one of the two strikers is involved.

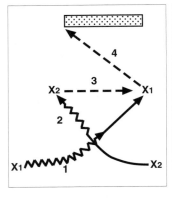

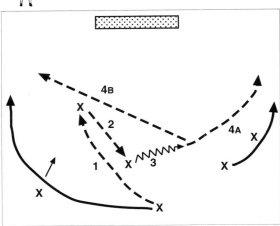

## Diagram 57: Takeover

Here a simple takeover is performed; the original dribbler spins off and receives a pass and takes a shot on goal.

## Diagram 58: Layoff to third man on.

Pass to target player with layoff to other striker who dribbles while an overlap takes place. Shown is one on each side but either one or the other is sufficient. Now player dribbles, generally across field because he doesn't need penetration, he just needs time in order to serve a pass to 4A or 4B the overlapping players. This frequently is the essence of an entire team attack.

Obviously anytime we have a capable dribbler and he finds himself 1v1 this simple option is still VERY POTENT. In any case the layoff, 1-2 move, takeover and the overlap are potent weapons for attaining strikes on goal. Since these basic combinations are potent all over the field for possession and penetration, train the entire team in these basic attacks on goal. In this way you accomplish finishing, penetration and possession - - this is economical training at its' best. Besides, players enjoy shooting exercises; this will keep team motivation at a peak.

# 8

# *Principles of Defense*

Yes, there is a defense, after offense! Defense may be half of the game, but should not comprise half of the instruction and practice time. Overemphasis on defense at an early age can hinder player development. This is not to advocate only attacking instruction for an entire season. At youth levels, every player should spend some time as a defender and a goalkeeper, and learn to take pride in these roles. But the young player must first concentrate on the technical and tactical skills of attack, (ball control, dribbling, passing, receiving, etc.). Then she can learn ways to play intelligently when the other team has the ball. This is only possible when a team has well-coordinated goals and communication, which requires maturity. This may occur around the age of thirteen, though it varies with the quality of players and the coaches' beliefs.

Whenever there are attacking and defending counter parts, the attacking instruction comes first. For example, first attacker instruction precedes first defender instruction, dribbling precedes tackling, offensive restarts precede defensive ones, and so on. Good defense will not exist until players are comfortable with the ball and encouraged to play offense. In fact, the quality of a team's defense cannot be tested until it faces a good offense.

The decision of defensive style (high pressure vs. low pressure, man-to-man vs. zonal) depends upon the immediate situation, the personnel, the particular third of the field, and the score. For example, a team that is behind in the score may play high pressure defense in order to regain possession; a team that is ahead in the score may opt for low pressure defense in order to protect its final third. Higher level teams are able to switch intelligently from one style to another to adapt to these variables.

Virtually all high level play combines man-to-man coverage

with zonal concepts. Therefore, the ability to play both man-to-man and zonal defense should be a primary defensive objective for the youth coach. This takes more than one season, but the benefits in terms of understanding and teamwork are well worth the effort. Defense is above all a mental disposition, where the mind drives the body.

Many young players intuitively mark tightly when they are close to the ball, and loosely when they are not. This is the first step toward zonal defense, and is easily developed in smallsided games. Encourage your players to loosely mark the attacker who is farthest from the ball. Then observe how these defenders cover the proper space. They should place themselves goal side, and be able to see their man and the ball.

Once again, the instruction integrates technique, principles of player roles, tactics, and finally, functional training. To progress immediately from technique to functional training hinders player development. This error leads to poor decision-making and lack of teamwork. It only reinforces blind clearing kicks and overcommitment by impatient defenders who are misled into thinking that their first objective is to win the ball. Such one-dimensional training creates one-dimensional players! It is much better to delay, then when you have cover you can be more aggressive in trying to win the ball.

In developing individual defensive skill, the many attacking activities previously described will expose players to most defensive situations. In these activities and smallsided games, coaches will be able to identify those players with the proper mental dispositions of good judgment, patience, and discipline. Such players can serve as models for the rest, since every player becomes a defender the moment possession is lost.

What these players seem to do intuitively may be consciously taught to other players: Stay on your feet. If cover is offered by a second attacker, win the ball; if not, keep the attacker from turning with the ball; if the attacker does turn, force a back or square pass, or shepherd him across the field or along the touchline. Protect the space behind you. Be patient! Do not tackle when the attacker has full control. The moment to tackle is when the attacker is half turned, or has just dribbled the ball and no longer has contact with it.

Tackling when the attacker has contact on the ball requires the defender's all out effort and weight behind the ball. In this case, lifting the ball over the attacker's foot will usually help.

These individual skills are the foundation of small group tactics. Together they are the key to quality defense, which is **team** defense. Once again, the principles of player roles are the cornerstone. The principles of first, second and third defenders, discussed in Chapter 1, may need review before we apply them in training. Note that these defensive roles correspond directly to attacking roles; that is, while the first attacker seeks to penetrate, the first defender tries to delay that penetration; the second attacker offers support to help the first attacker, whereas the second defender offers cover to help the first defender. Similarly, third attackers try to lend width and depth, while third defenders attempt to restrict space.

A glance at diagram #1 in Chapter 1 reveals that the two triangles (attackers and defenders) do not mirror each other. This is because intelligent defense is not simply a strict man-to-man proposition. True, the first defenders, in applying pressure to the ball, can be said to play man-to-man. But the second and third defenders, in **covering an area and a man**, often use a partial zonal defense.

Even the best-intentioned parents and coaches are often unaware of this, and encourage all defenders to mark tightly at the wrong times. Indeed, the central issue of confusion in defending appears to focus on marking. Frequently, players on the field are making better defensive decisions than the instruction shouted from the touchlines. The second and third defenders often should not mark up tight! Strict man-to-man coverage permits the attack to determine the location of all players. Thus, the attack can take a strong defender away from vital space, exploit 1v1 situations, or crowd one area in order to open another. Against a smart attack, strict man-to man marking can actually reduce pressure on the ball, and eliminate cover and balance, thus preventing the defense from executing its major defensive objectives.

Even in a man-to-man defense, defenders should not mark tightly when they are outnumbered. As obvious as it sounds, two defenders cannot cover three attackers who are spread out. Tight marking in this case results in allowing one attacker space to penetrate, simply by reducing the 3v2 to a 2v1. Thus there is a need for players, coaches, and spectators to first and foremost understand the roles of first, second and third defenders. Only then will be concept of zonal coverage make full sense, and misdirection from the touchlines subside. Naturally, when the freeback is free of man coverage, there is cover. In such a case, defenders can work more tightly.

Zonal coverage in soccer applies the concepts of first, second, and third defender roles to specific areas of the field and specific situations. It also relates to the attacking principle of four man width across the field, which calls for at least that many defenders, and preferably more. Three man width is never enough for a solid defense in the defending third; that number of players could not adequately defend the vital area in front of the goal. Two attackers would find it easy to get to the central area and beat the lone central defender with a 2v1. Even a single strong attacker becomes a great threat, especially as more young players develop the skill and confidence to take on defenders. Three man width diminishes the vital factors of pressure on the ball, cover, and concentration. It invariably reduces the defense to a man-to-man style, which is only as strong as its weakest link.

Again, 3 designated defenders does not mean the goal is defended by 3 players. It may be 4, but frequently it is 5,6 or even 10, especially on corner kicks and other dead ball situations.

Four man width, on the other hand, enables a team to maxi-mize the defensive principles of delay, cover, and concentra-tion. With four man width, two defenders can cover the cen-tral area no matter where the ball goes. This gives depth to the defense. If the ball changes fields rapidly, they can remain in the vital area while another defender puts pressure on the ball. Even if five attackers come forward, the defense still has a reasonable chance of denying a goal. Even if the free defend-er is forced to mark, there remains some form of cover which allows for reasonable defensive safety.

If four man defensive width is good, is a five man defense better? Perhaps at higher levels, but not at the youth level. This would diminish the number of players committed to attack, and along with it the appropriate support and realiza-tion of success. It would distort the sense of offensive bal-ance. In short, the quality and enjoyment of the game would suffer. Of course, encourage midfielders, even forwards, to chase back when needed.

In the final third, therefore, the defense must maintain four man width, with concentrated defense of the most vital areas, as in the diagram below, where the wingbacks have more area to cover than the centerbacks.

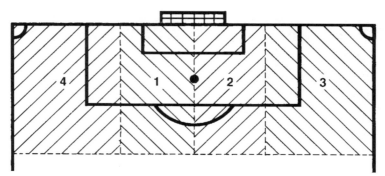

**Diagram #59: This is alot of ground to protect, so even when we only designate 3 defenders, one midfielder knows his first responsibility is defense.**

This coverage is generally considered the bare minimum, even for brief periods of time. When the attack involves more than four players, man-to-man marking may become impossi-ble, and zonal coverage becomes mandatory. The first defensive principle of delay, with pressure on the ball, proves more vital than ever in this situation. Delay allows time for more defenders to recover and help. For reasonably sound defense, however, the team objective should always be to outnumber the attackers, especially in the defensive third.

Frequently, against only 2 strikers teams use only 3 DESIGNATED defenders, but in this case one midfielder is often a designated defending midfielder who generally stays a bit behind the remaining midfielders. Of course, mobility among strikers, midfielders and defenders is high level soccer. Infact nowadays we not only emphasize a total soccer player, but we are more interested in a good SHAPE to defend and attack, instead of a player being in a rigid position. All combinations demand changes in player positions, and combo's always represent good soccer, but the team must still maintain a good SHAPE. This is as true for defense, as it is for offense, may be even more so!

But the real challenge to a defense occurs when the attack is numbers up. This situation forces decision-making and teamwork by the defense, and takes time. To accelerate this development, defensive techniques and tactics can be integrated in the next drill, adapted from the popular basketball drill where a 3v2 in one direction is immediately followed by a 2v1 counterattack. This drill is repeated quickly and intensely to force defensive decision-making in a numbers down situation. Keep some extra balls in each net. Here's how it works in grids or on half of a soccer field with full-size traditional goals or flat faced Wiel Coerver goals.

Three attackers face two defenders, as in the diagrams below. Player O1, on the middle, attacks one goal directly. One defender must mark him, and the second must offer some cover. In a short time (two 40 minute sessions), the three attackers will score at will, especially it they can reduce the 3v2 to a 2v1. The defenders may need to be alerted to this tactic, and try not to be drawn away from vital attacking space.

Once a shot is taken or possession is lost, D1 and D2 attack the opposite goal. Now O1 becomes the lone defender, as in diagram #61. This is a simple 2v1, but emphasis can be placed on one of several areas: the training from attack to defense and vice versa, positioning, tackling, etc. This 2v1 will culminate in a shot or loss of possession.

Immediately, D1, D2 and O1 join together and attack the opposite goal. This time, O2 and O3 become defenders to form a 3v2. See diagram #62.

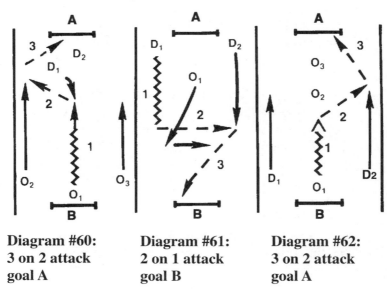

| Diagram #60: | Diagram #61: | Diagram #62: |
|---|---|---|
| 3 on 2 attack | 2 on 1 attack | 3 on 2 attack |
| goal A | goal B | goal A |

In this drill, the rapid transitions from attack to defense challenges players to employ the principles of player roles in a constantly changing situation. Delay, pressure on the ball, and zonal play can be further refined if defenders learn to use the offside rule to their advantage, without becoming too flat. Good defensive coaching inculcates the importance of keeping the ball in front of the defenders. But once beaten, the defender can still help by immediate chase to get goal side. This may force immediate chase to get goal side. This may force the attacker to an early or hurried decision.

From this drill to shortsided games emphasizing defensive positioning and decision-making is a very short step. Encourage communication among defenders, especially from the second defender; the player in this role needs to let the first defender know that there is cover. This facilitates shepherding and tackling, and discourages the attacker from trying to take on two defenders.

The next stage of development is team defense, which hinges upon the particular third of the field and the final four. In defense, the safety/risk ratio in each third remains the same as on attack: strikers can take risks to regain possession in the attacking third, midfielders balance safety and risk, while the final four plays mainly for safety to protect the space behind them. In general, there is tight marking in the final third by the final four defenders and some midfielders. Meanwhile, strikers and some midfielders lay a zone to cover midfield. Of course, defenders must work very hard while the ball is moving.

At this point, it should be made clear that only two systems of play are recognized here. The 4-3-3 is advocated because it is a simple system that aids development and represents the most ideal balance of any team arrangement. The 4-4-2, with the extra midfielder, is a useful system later on for youth because it fosters direct attack, high pressure, and transition opportunities.

There are many wonderful systems, but this book is about the neglected **basic foundation material upon which systems are formulated.** Once the basic principles are understood, formulating good systems is easy. What does not work is substituting systems in lieu of the basic player roles knowledge. When this happens, systems discussion are nothing more than a substitute (excuse) for learning the basic principles of the game of soccer.

As often as possible, we would like to stop the ball and regain possession before it reaches our final four. This requires players with the drive to get back very quickly when the ball is lost, and the anticipation to cut out passes. Back peddling and constant movement, even if it is only walking, are of great value, and need to be encouraged.

With these prerequisites, midfielders (or forwards) can then put high pressure on the opposing team and regain possession with some frequency. Even occasional success here would be a great help to a team's total effort. A quality defense requires strikers and support players who have learned how to play defense. They must especially realize the importance of chase, attempting to get behind the ball, as well as where and when their efforts will pay the greatest dividend.

Strikers must be more responsible for regaining possession in their striking third, even if this is only occasional. This is true if for no other reason than to force a keeper to kick a long 50/50 ball. But as long as the ball is in the striking third, no matter which team possesses, strikers must play at full effort for high pressure defense to succeed. Loss of possession should not mean a rest for the strikers. In this third, forcing a flat pass, especially close to the penalty area, is also a very helpful tactic; the interception of such a pass in the striking third could well provide a good shot on goal. Furthermore, strikers should enjoy the luxury of risk tackling. Defenders cannot afford to be on the ground, but a striker can risk a tackle, due to the number of players behind him and the distance from his own goal. Of course, when strikers are defending in the defending third, they must be more cautious, emphasizing delay as well as pressure on the ball.

Another high pressure tactic used by defensive strikers and midfielders involves setting a trap to regain possession and win a transition goal. The defending players allow the ball to go to a wingback, then close down on him with two players. Other defenders position themselves to deny a pass, as in diagram #63.

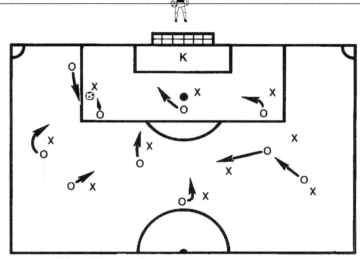

**Diagram #63: High pressure trap.**

This is even more productive when the attacking wingback is close to the touchline, as the out-of-bounds is used to tighten the trap. Two defenders could get toe to toe, thus depriving the attacker from dribbling or passing. The extra defender for this trap is obtained by leaving the furthest attacker from the ball free. In the case illustrated below, it would be the attacking left wing or some player in the shaded area.

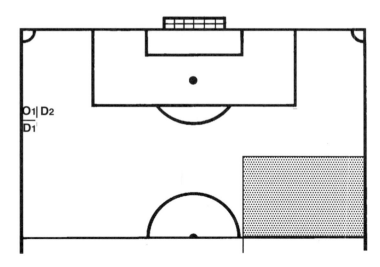

**Diagram #64: Undefended area with two players attempting to totally dispossess O1 from the ball.**

To succeed with such traps, strikers must feint a withdrawal; then after the keeper has released the ball to a defender, they must make an all-out effort. Unless they sell this fake withdrawal, the keeper will merely kick the ball long. These high pressure tactics require good conditioning, mental toughness, and awareness through coaching. To support these defensive strikers, the midfield 'engine room' fosters quality tactics through using fitness for aggressive cover.

The major defensive task of midfielders is to prevent the opponent from moving the ball through midfield. Intelligent team defense will force the ball square or back. If pressure from a defensive midfielder forces a long forward pass, this may also work for the defense: many long hurried passes are 50/50 balls. Even if these passes are directed toward a teammate, the defense is facing the play and gains an advantage. On the other hand, midfielders who remain in striking positions when not actively engaged in the strike can easily cause a total team breakdown.

Of course, in a low pressure defense, these tactics would change radically. There would be less chance of regaining the ball in the striking third or in midfield because all or almost all players are withdrawing. In fact, low pressure calls for either no pressure or only token pressure in the striking third. To develop this style of defense, players can practice falling back to the midfield line on the full field and not trying to win the ball. The coach merely directs the players to proper locations. The ball can be carried by the players or the coach. This type of activity must be brief, and only used with very accomplished players over age thirteen.

A combination of high and low pressure is common nowadays. This involves a very strong effort to regain the ball as soon as it is lost. If this fails the entire team withdraws to defend in its own half of the field. Good teams are capable of low, high or combinational pressure.

Coming to the final third, let us continue our discussion of team defense with the most common situation: four defenders against three strikers. In this case, where the attackers are so widely spread, the stopper is marking the opposing central striker, and the two wingback are marking the wings (see diagram #65). This is slightly different from our model diagram in Chapter 1 because the numerical advantage allows the freeback to take the second defender's major responsibility; that is, he offers cover to the first defender without also having to mark the second attacker.

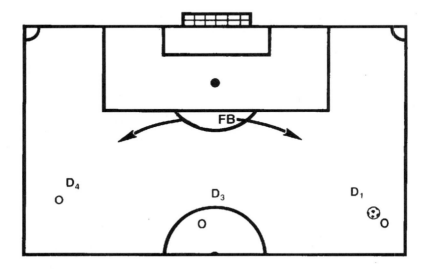

**Diagram #65: Free defender offering cover.**

Of course, if another attacker overlaps, that player becomes the responsibility of the freeback (see diagram #66), or a switch may be called. Any further attacking players must be picked up by midfielders; otherwise, the final four must switch to a zonal defense.

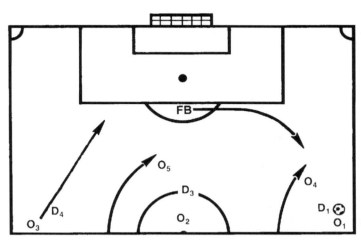

**Diagram #66: Free defender marking the overlapping attacker.**

One of the most obvious dangers is the freeback committing too early, which could allow another overlapping player to go to goal unmarked. Therefore it is important that the freeback be an intelligent decision-maker and a strong communicator. Any player who desires to master the roles of first, second, and third defender should spend extra time at this position. Allowing O5 free access is dangerous.

To develop team coherence in the defending third, short-sided games with specific limitations can be very useful. Full-size portable goals on a field about the size of two penalty areas will allow for realistic problem-solving. Goalies can be added, and the field enlarged to include some midfielders. As always, reward good decision-making and teamwork on the part of the defense. One or two servers can be added to create a numbers up attack, but at first these servers may be limited to their defensive half. Other variations could include scoring a point for every good verbal direction from the freeback, for every successful trap, or for every time the ball is forced square or back.

Freeze activity is another useful approach during these games. One freeze of less than a minute of instruction for each five minutes of play is appropriate. More instruction than that destroys the natural flow of the game, and becomes boring. Players can learn from a lot of playing, and a little talking! The game itself is a great teacher.

Three final defenders is not very different, since this is often employed against only two strikers. Therefore, there still is a free defensive player. The one difference with the 3 man back is that the roles are very interchangeable - - at any given moment any 2 of the 3 could be marking, whereas with the 4 man back a far greater attempt is made to keep the sweeper free of marking responsibilities.

These games will foster the development of a proud and cohesive final four with the proper mental disposition for defense: drive, communication, teamwork, and good decision making. While quality defense is a team effort, it is neverthe-less built upon individual skills and the knowledge of defensive roles. This also pertains to the defending of the goal and to defending against free kicks, as we will see in the next chapters.

There is no suggestion of preference of man-to-man vs, zonal play. However, in World Cup 1994 seventeen teams played zones, one team played man-to-man, and six teams played combinational defenses.

Because second defender cover can be awfully poor in terms of player development in strict man-to-man systems, I do advocate some zonal instruction, if for no other reason to fully develop the second defender responsibilities of cover.

*Note how the keeper is leaning into the save and keeping the ball "IN-FRONT." This is a major point in all keeping instruction.*

*Outside the foot bent ball pass or shot technique is being developed. Notice how the player will be able to continue his run in order to receive a return pass. Outside of the foot allows deception and can be delivered quite far. The modern game demands a RUN to receive in order to create defensive chaos after passing.*

*This header was driven to the ground by the FOREHEAD in line (laterally) with the keeper. Needless to say this ball was not saved. Not seen was a good curvature of the spine with the visible arm thrust to attain the good power that was acheived.*

*Ball is thrown at wall with player facing the wall and the player must quickly react (catch) the ball. REACTION SPEED, W-catch and leaning into a save are all emphasized. This activity alternates the regular ball with the medicine ball (10 trials each). The medicine ball is used to develop finger STRENGTH.*

*Two players wrestle for the ball in order to develop STRENGTH. The best of ten is a winner of a single set. The best of three sets is the day's winner.*

*While we frequently want the keeper to join field players to develop better collection and passing skills, we also want field players to join keepers. Here the whole team has joined the keepers to develop FLEX- IBILITY, in what is frequently considered a typical keeper activity.*

*Here the keeper is working on quick ACCURATE DISTRIBUTION to field players. He is using obstacle course markers as a target and the delivery is a line drive to a wingback.*

*Here the keeper is working QUICK FOOTWORK and MULTIPLE SAVES. This is a very economical activity further involving fitness, catching, distribution, vision, and coordinated work with his stopper and free back. Ball distance, angles, and speed can all be varied to increase the total value of this fun activity.*

When practice sessions range from only one to three times a week no single practice can be without playing the actual game of soccer. Sometimes it may be a full scrimmage but more often it is a SHORT-SIDED game with restrictions coordinated to the day's instruction. Here the flat faced goals were used and the boys are showing offensive support AND good defensive cover.

The four goals (Dutch Gates) activities encourage change of field (change in POINT of ATTACK). Here the lesson is not lost as there are available MOBILITY players. The defense has pressure on the ball, cover and balance. Well done!

*The boys are playing 5v5 with keepers (anything from 1v1 to 6v6 is acceptable) on full sized goals. However, 4 v 4 or more is clearly more match related. Shots, STRIKING RUNS, and DEFENDING in the immediate goal area can only be refined with a great deal of experience (repetition). This type of activity with goals 40-70 yards apart is a must!*

*In 1v1v1v1vK the striker gets to TAKE ON one player at a time and then place a shot past the keeper. Initial stages of this activity have defenders semi-active (crab defenders for players age 7-11), but later on this is done with full defensive effort.*

*Players are all in a grid in pairs. Here the emphasis was communication involving EYE CONTACT and ACCELERATED RUNS to receive the ball. Fitness and passing technique are a natural part of this warm-up activity.*

*Team tactics instructions involves brief explanation, walk through, performance with token pressure, HANDOUT of the tactic, and use of the tactic in games or full scrimmage. The handout allows absentees to "keep up to date," allows for questions, serves as a visual reminder for players to look back to, and keeps team organization CLEAR.*

*Flat face goals triple the REPETITION of a technique in a given time frame. Here full volleys are being taken as the coach serves balls over the top. The coach demands shots under the 4' rope pictured to emphasize LOW SHOTS. Players follow their shot and also run around the cone before returning for the next trial so that fitness is incorporated.*

*This coach is PREPARED. He carries all this in his convenient big bag. Balls, cones, obstacle course markers, scrimmage vests, medicine kit, and coaching board with his written plan. Some coaches will need a net as all practices require a net on goal. The TEAM treasury made this possible. Each player still brings water and a ball.*

*DEHYDRATION is a concern of safety. Water breaks are needed, especially in warm weather, overtime games, tournaments involving more than one game per day and of course for rigorous training sessions. Remember water is still needed in colder weather and rainy days. Also, thirst is not always an accuarte indicator of the need for fluids.*

*WARMING up is of prime importance. In general this means some form of running with the ball such as dribbling, or moving, passing/receiving activities. Stretching after warm-up or in conjunction with the warm-up is also important. These players have not forgotten the neck area, which is important as major catastrophies frequently involve the carotid artery.*

*This is a CONTINUOUS MOTION activity in which a diagonal pass is followed by a square pass in a 1-2 MOVEMENT with a SHOT on goal. Players simply go from one goal to the next in a circular fashion obtaining many repetitions in a short period of time. Fitness in incorporated.*

*Here the player is working between a rebounder and a flat faced goal. A wall would also work. Excellent for turning ball; involving both ground and air balls. Obviously this solo work prefects technique.*

*Among the teams that introduced and kept soccer alive in the United States were college teams such as Huntly Parker's Eagles at Brockport. Today's players are more skillful but they couldn't teach this group about enthusiasm or fitness. Many are still coaching today and Huntly himself is in the Soccer Hall of Fame.*

*Equipment was crude by today's standards, but apparently there was no lack of grace in those earlier periods. Guess Who?*

*The indoor game helps develop speed, ball control, working in small areas, shielding and of course aides fitness. One must use the indoor game in a MINDFUL MANNER if it is to help the outdoor game. That is, gain from its strengths and avoid its dangers.*

The U.S.S.F. and N.S.C.A.A. coaching schools provide periods of heightened learning which is nearly impossible to gain in any other way. This one is part of the National Soccer Coaches Association of C.W. Post College in July 1985. Starting with the fourth person in rear row from left to right instructors are: Doug May, Jeff Tipping, Jim Lennox (Director), and Ron McEachen.

*Travel in soccer helps to develop the mind as well as the body. This 'sad' group from New York is pictured in front of their touring bus in California. The Great Game's international flavor is educational and enjoyable.*

# 9

## *Keeper Instruction Techniques and Decision-Making*

Goalkeeper development is the most neglected area of youth soccer. In a typical team practice, the keeper is virtually ignored; yet, in a typical match, he receives much or all the blame for a goal. There is no justification for this. The only solution is to concentrate on the needs of the goalkeeper, and spend more time on his development. Coaches may fear that this time takes too much away from the field players, but if we agree that keeper instruction is vital, we will find ways to meet this need. Few coaches are fortunate enough to have a keeper coach or assistant, so most youth coaches need some separate sessions with their goalies. Sometime before or after the regular session is excellent. Any time spent in recruiting an experienced keeper for one or two sessions is well spent. This chapter will offer a teachable framework, with successful approaches that combine keeper training with field training.

The keeper must function as part of a team; anything that unduly separates him from the field players may harm team unity. The current vogue for excessive flair, unusual dress, overly large gloves, and a permissive attitude on the part of keepers only undermines this cohesion. As Joe Machnik says, "The goalkeeper really is No. 1, but must always prove it by performance."

State-of-the-art goalkeeper instruction emphasizes the similarities, rather than the differences, between this position and any field position. This is because the keeper, like any other player, must make decisions and protect the space behind him. In this context, footwork is of vital importance. After all, the keeper must cover ground, change direction, leap, dive, dribble, and kick; all this requires as much footwork as a field player. Therefore the goalie should be first and foremost a soccer player, capable of all field techniques and tactics. At the youth level, every field player should be given keeper instruction and experience, and every player who wants only to be a goalie should first become a field player. Without field experience, a goalie is tactically impoverished.

Like all defenders, keepers need the proper mental disposition, especially a positive outlook regarding their ability to deny goals. They must exemplify mental toughness. Keepers often see all goals as saveable and a result of their own error, though this is a fallacy. Nevertheless, this attitude frequently causes them to try to rectify all causes of goals. As long as this personal responsibility outlook remains positive, this can be a great asset to any team. In addition, keepers must be highly motivated to work independently at times. (A team should have at least two keepers, who work together and push each other.)

The notion that keepers must be 'crazy', weird, or very different is totally false. Yes, they must have great courage, but that does not mean that they must be fool hardy. This courage must be accompanied by excellent judgment and technique. Coaches should select keepers with this in mind.

Furthermore, keepers can be any personality type. Their behavior can be natural to whatever personality they possess. We must not confuse seriousness with solemnity nor humor with irresponsibility. Whatever type of personality, it is essential that the field players have confidence in their goalie.

Physically goalies should be good athletes and also be extremely agile. Size is not critical, but quickness ability is. Keepers should know the height of their vertical jump, and train to increase it. Total fitness, flexibility, agility, power and leaping ability are great assets. Good hands are an absolute must. Training with a bounceable medicine ball will dramatically enhance strength, toughness, and technique. See the appendix article "Using the Medicine Ball in Developing Technique."

As in overall player instruction, the starting point is technique and decision-making. For safety reasons, technique is very important for goalies. But these techniques are only as good as the decisions of how and when to use them.

Therefore, as they learn to catch, box, dive, throw, and kick, they must at the same time learn to apply these skills intelligently to the game. The foundation, of course, is to understand and implement the principles of player roles. As the final defender, keepers must be thoroughly aware of the roles of first, second, and third defenders. As the first attacker, they must also know the roles of first, second, and third attackers. Only then will they understand what is happening on the field, and be able to link with the rest of the team. This reinforces the keepers' need for field experience.

Like any field player, the keeper becomes the first attacker when he has the ball, and will try to penetrate with a good pass. When a wingback has the ball, the keeper may become the second attacker, offering support. Similarly, the goalie becomes the first defender on a breakaway and must protect the space, the goal, behind him. Covering for fullbacks, the keeper becomes the second defender. The point is, that the keeper is bound by the same principles as the field players.

The goalie is first and foremost a decision-maker, and these decisions are crucial. Therefore, every keeper training session must concentrate on the major areas of decision-making; namely, **breakaways**, **crosses**, and **dead** ball situations. Here 'breakaway' is used in its broadest sense, meaning when the final defender is beat. In the following progressions, alternate two or more keepers. Encourage them to maintain a positive rivalry.

The **breakaway** is an exciting play that not only tests keepers' decisions, but also their courage. Prior knowledge of the attacker is a great help in the decision, but timing is the key in all cases. The single most important element is to be in the **'Get Set'** position when the shot is taken. The keeper is no longer moving. Even if his angle position is not perfect, he must get ready to react to the shot. Therefore, he must be balanced on both feet, able to move in any direction. The feet are shoulder width apart, the weight is on the toes, knees are bent, and hands partially extended at the sides. The attacker should start from different distances (from 10 to 35 yards) and different angles. In order to see all the various types of attackers, a different player should be used in this training. Some attackers try power, others chips, some like low shots, others favor the corners. Goalies should be taught how to deal with each particular shot and angle, as well as inswingers and outswingers.

Repeated power dives to save the ball off the attacker's foot must be performed. At first the attacker should be passive, allowing the keepers to save 100% of the time. Gradually, the attacker becomes more active and imaginative. Decision-making involves making the save before, during, or after the attacker plays the ball. The earlier the save can be made, the better the chance of success; this is where timing comes in. If the attacker is dribbling, the timing is the same as in a foot tackle: the moment to win the ball is when the attacker has just played it and no longer has contact with it.

Possibly, the weakest area for keepers is pre-assessment of the opposing players. It is beneficial to attend to styles, moves, speed, strengths, and weaknesses of opponents throughout a match. Knowing if a player is a one touch shooter or a several touch controller can be useful in deciding how to handle a breakaway.

As the attacker approaches, keepers should steer the player to a location that they know they can cover, the near post. Tactical points involve studying the attacker's degree of control, speed, and the distance the ball is from the feet.

Of course, keepers should also be schooled in 2vK, 2v1+K, 3v2, etc., but these situations can be attended to after the keeper learns how to deal with 1vK. In the case of 2vK, the tactic is the same as a field player defending the 2v1: eliminate the likelihood of a pass to the second attacker (delay without allowing the first attacker to shoot), then play 1v1 against the first attacker. From here, the progression is the same as those of field players; gradually add another attacker at less than full effort until the keeper has mastered the tactic. Then increase the effort to challenge the keepers' decision-making, quickness, reach, and technique. As always, it is best to work up to a smallsided game, using full-size goals in a small field or grids.

The second major area is **crosses**. Beginning with dead ball crosses, the training should involve balls to be caught, boxed, parried, deflected, and, when too far away, left for a field player. Keepers are placed in the proper decision-making environment, and technique is perfected in this environment.

With these crosses, begin with a single receiver. Work up to body contact gradually. As keepers gain confidence and are no longer intimidated by being jostled, add more receivers. Progress to a game of four or even more attackers versus four defenders. However, be certain that there is <u>an abundance of simple activity involving the decision of whether or not to leave the line.</u> Before more complex activities can be attempted, keepers must be able to read the flight of the ball and make a good decision to deal with it.

In this way keepers will learn how to attack a ball that has four or five players who are attempting to control it. To deal with his own teammates, he must be decisive, clear, and simple. Two commands are fundamental: usually keepers will call out with authority "Keeper!" for any ball that they will attack, and "Away!" for any ball that a teammate must handle. Some coaches use only one verbal command, "Keeper!" or silence.

As instruction progresses, the crosses can come from an active dribbler. This forces movement even before the cross occurs. The dribbler should cross from all parts of the area shown in the diagram below.

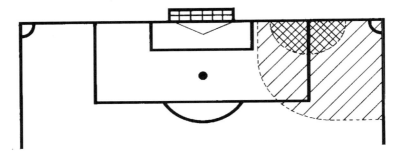

**Diagram #67: The closer to goal the cross comes from, the more difficult it is for the defense.**

Crosses from the darker shaded area warrant additional practice, since these are especially dangerous. The same is true for high floating balls that can cause indecision. In both cases, these crosses should come from the left as well as right side of the field.

Generally, the major decision is whether to make an all-out effort to save or to stay close to the goal line. During these workouts, ask the keepers questions about why and when they decided to leave the line. Once it is known how they make decisions, they can be taught additional or more relevant criteria for these decisions. The coach and the keepers should work very closely to solve such problems together. This requires a coach's concerted effort to get to know the keeper's individual personality, learning style, and self-image. While this approach is very helpful with all players, it becomes essential with goalies.

The technical aspect of handling crosses includes back peddling, side stepping, maintaining good balance with weight on balls of the feet, hand out in front and maintaining vision. Of course, all catching skills must be executed with perfect technique. Keepers must train at 100% effort on every play until the ball is safely in their hands. The area of multiple saves is also important in these situations. The next step is to add distribution targets for the keeper, as was illustrated in

Chapter V.

The third area of decision-making is **dead ball situations**. The major reason for failure in this area lies in communication, because the field players do not set up on time or mark properly. As a result, a good shot becomes the goal which cannot be saved by the keeper. While keepers do not necessarily set the wall, good keepers are certain that whoever sets the wall does so quickly and correctly. Once field players cover the near post properly, have the correct numbers in the wall, and mark the attackers, then saving decisions by goalies become much easier. Young keepers generally cannot pro - tect the entire goal; therefore, an additional player or two can be placed in goal to at least cover the lower portions near the posts.

All dead ball situations must be simulated, practiced, and discussed. While many such situations, like defending direct and indirect kicks, call for the entire team, others require only half, or even two or three players. In these cases, the coach has other activities for the uninvolved players. During a water break, a keeper can remain in goal, and some players can practice their techniques, such as penalty kicks, corner kicks, and throw-ins in the final third. All have a water break, but not necessarily altogether.

The recommended practice plan calls for work on special situations during each session. Goalies can follow the same plan, substituting (or adding) keeper tactics and techniques for those of the field player. The order of activities is as follows:

     1. warm-up and stretch;
     2. teach a basic tactic with related technique;
     3. shortsided work involving that tactic;
     4. special situation;
     5. scrimmage.

Note that the sedentary activity of a special situation offers a break between two high aerobic activities. One fifteen minute session on a single situation (indirect kicks, corner kicks, etc.) is ideal, as it provides a physical rest and does not become boring. If possible, the special situation of the day should relate to that day's tactic and technique.

Another defensive situation that calls for excellent

communication is the offside trap. Although this is frequently orchestrated by the freeback or centerback, keepers have additional input, especially when the trap is close to the goal. Keepers can see all players, and generally have time to assess the opponent's attack. Thus, if goalies want to remove the trap, they communicate this to the freeback or centerback. Such moment to moment adjustments involve the directing final defender and the keeper. The decision to remove the trap for the entire game or half, however, usually comes from the coach.

Since keepers can usually see the whole field throughout the game, they are in a good position to help their team by proper distribution and commands. Intelligent distribution sets a pattern, and places keepers in close teamwork with the final four. This concept is important to a unified team defense.

Decision-making continues to be the thrust of goalie training even when they have made a save and are ready to distribute. At this point the keeper becomes the first attacker, looking to penetrate, or at least to maintain safe possession in the defending third. Therefore, the workouts should provide for choices of where and how to distribute. In these situations, the question of where should be answered first, since the distance and accuracy required for the distribution will dictate whether the ball is rolled, thrown, or kicked. Usually the ball is delivered to the side opposite from where the shot came, since this is generally the weak side where there are the fewest opponents.

Lack of training in communication and teamwork among keepers and field players causes most youth keepers to blindly punt the ball for distance. Proper coaching of the final four and the midfield will alleviate this, allowing for better distribution by the keeper, and better reception by the field players. Chapter V elucidates these tactics and techniques for field players. Now let us look at keeper skills in distribution.

For a short or medium length precise pass, goalies can <u>roll the ball</u> to the receiver's feet or to safe space in front of the receiver. The ball should have sufficient pace (depending on the receiver's technical skill) and a moderate top spin so as to maintain its course. This also helps to keep the ball near the ground for rapid collection. The stance should be like a boxer, one foot in front of the other, with bent knees. The release should not be too high because this can cause needless bouncing, which reduces velocity and increases difficulty in collecting. Too low a release is only a problem on a poor field (rough ground or very deep turf). Upon release, finger tips should be on the ball, and fingers spread apart (but not to maximum, as this can cause tightness in the fingers).

Medium passes can be thrown side-arm or overhead. The emphasis is on accuracy. Young keepers can cradle the ball between fingers and forearm. The overhead release may be more accurate. The side-arm release tends to curve the pass.

Long passes can be punted or drop-kicked; these, of course, will lack the accuracy of the other techniques, but are useful in taking the pressure off the defense. Goalies should be made to realize that long punts and drop-kicks can be 50/50 balls; therefore, they should be used judiciously. **Such passes should have a target in mind**. Practice will improve accuracy; perfect the technique first, then add power. Developing players should serve by dropping the ball using **both hands**. Whether the kicking leg snaps at the knee or remains straight is an individual choice. In either case, goalies should try both methods.

With each distribution, keepers must maintain vision of the ball while retreating to the goal area. Retreating techniques include back-pedaling and side stepping, so both must be practiced to improve quickness. These are great conditioning exercises as well. With the goalie on the line, serve a ball that requires a 10-15 yard run to reach. Once the save is made, the keeper can return the ball to the server (or distribute to a field player), then back pedal to goal, keeping one hand up and ready. While returning to goal another serve can be made.

Keepers can now begin to concentrate on positioning, which is extremely important to the overall quality of goalkeeping. The rule of thumb is quite simple: Keepers occupy a spot in the penalty area in proportion to the location of the ball on the whole field. Thus, when the ball is in the opponent's penalty box, they should be at the edge of their own penalty area; when the ball is at midfield, they are nine yards from the goal line; when the ball is in their own penalty box, they are nearly on the goal line. The next diagram illustrates this by linking various positions of the ball with corresponding positions of the keeper.

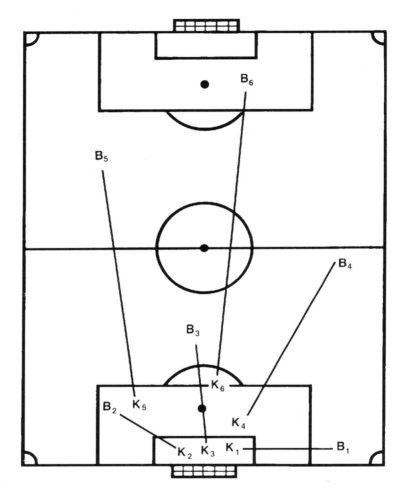

**Diagram #68: Basic keeper positioning is important to the overall quality of keeping.**

This movement also helps keepers to concentrate on the game even when the ball is in the opponent's end. But the intention is foremost to increase the amount of space that the keeper can protect. The further keepers can come off their line, and still protect the space behind them, the more effective they will be. Of course, that amount of space varies with the individual athlete, but advanced goalie training works to increase that area.

This instruction will help keepers to maintain sensible positions even prior to the major decisions of position changes to stop an attack. For young goalkeepers, our main concern in position play is when the opponent is in scoring range. To clarify these various positions, a cone can be placed three yards out from center of goal. This is a good location for a young keeper to learn how to assess angles and a good guide to indicate how far out to go. For example, when the ball is at point B2 in the diagram below, the keeper should come out to the imaginary line between the post and the cone, at a point where the near post is protected. In other words, the keeper is at the perpendicular of a triangle formed by an imaginary line extending from each goal post to a point three yards out from the center of the goal.

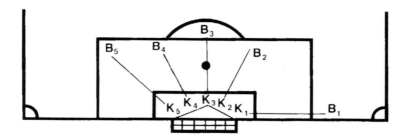

**Diagram #69: Proper positioning in goalmouth area.**

All dives cover the near post with the hands, while the far post area is covered with the feet. This helps to deflect shots past the outside of the post, thereby reducing the danger of a goal. While goalies must dive, the better ones have to dive less often, since their superior position play allows them to make easier saves. The mark of good goalies, then, is not how well they dive, but how seldom they are forced to dive.

Another way to help young keepers to visualize angle play

is to tie each end of a long rope to the goalpost, forming a tri-angle at various points in the penalty area. The rope will vividly show the limits of the ball's path toward goal, and the width of that angle can be bisected by the goalie, again favoring the near post. The imaginary bisector is the direct path to the ball. The goalie will begin to realize the tactical advantage of narrowing that angle by moving toward the ball. As the location of the angle changes, the keeper will learn to adjust his position accordingly.

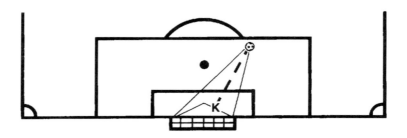

**Diagram #70:  Movement in front of the goal.**

These exercises must be expanded into smallsided games which will force keepers to concentrate on all aspects of the game. The coach can award points for each save, each good distribution, each good decision on position, and so forth. Finally, a full-sided game will enable the keeper to put it all together with the entire team.

Perhaps more than any other player, the keeper will be able to assess the strengths and weaknesses of his game performance. This will form the agenda for a subsequent practice. In answering the question, "How were goals scored?" the keeper will learn to communicate with the final four, particularly in keeping the box uncrowded and the attack away from the goal.

In conclusion, all field players should take a turn at goalkeeping, and all goalkeepers should be field players. If nothing else field players will realize the visual confusion that the goalie faces when an attack occurs. The development of keepers combines technical instruction simultaneously with decision-making, then places goalies in a learning environment to practice both technique and decision-making on breakaways (1vs1), crosses, and special situations. In addition, keepers must develop skill in **communication**, especially with the final four defenders. The next chapter, in dealing with special situations, will offer specific suggestions for improvement in this area.

**Attempt to do the great preponderance of keeper training in the goal area - - after all, saving goals is not academic or merely technical, it is keeping the ball out of the net! To this end, perfect technique will not help if the keeper has not learned through experience the proper place to be. While poor technique is not encouraged, many a save <u>can</u> <u>be</u> <u>accomplished</u> <u>by</u> <u>merely</u> <u>being</u> in the correct location (by having made a good decision).**

# 10

## *Special Situations*

Free kicks and corner kicks account for a significant percentage of goals. Therefore they should be practiced from both offensive and defensive standpoints. These areas are often incorrectly addressed in youth soccer, mainly due to very young children participating in full size matches before they understand the rules and restarts. In this chapter, there is no intention to fully treat all aspects of this topic; we will merely present a few basic principles and deal with the more common errors and misconceptions.

While regular instruction in restarts is necessary, these sessions should be for short periods of time, fifteen minutes or less. Any longer instructional period for these rather sedentary activities becomes counterproductive. The time to teach special situations is between two rigorous activities, such as shortsided work and scrimmaging.

Since attacking instruction precedes defending instruction, it is important to follow this model in relation to special situations. There are no new skills needed here; therefore the emphasis is on tactics. Like the rest of the game, special situation tactics adjust according to the third of the field.

Let us suppose that our team is awarded the ball in our own defending third. Since a free kick does not present an immediate scoring threat at this distance, the opponents will not use a wall; instead, they will mark players and/or space to begin defending while they are in transition from attack to defense, (we are switching from defense to attack.) The tactical advantage will go to which ever team makes the most rapid transition. If we can put the ball into play very quickly, we can perhaps penetrate before they reorganize. A long pass may take several lax defenders out of the play. Therefore, our practice session works on quick organization and counterattack.

The opponent may use one man to encroach upon the ball in order to delay the free kick. Though this is contrary to the spirit of the game, it happens all too frequently at every level. Coaches would do well to alleviate this transgression before the game with a quick conference with the referee. At any rate, the encroachment forces a decision: whether to call for ten yards, thereby submitting to the delay, or whether to put the ball into play quickly, which means passing around the encroacher.

Because of coaching or poor modeling, most young players are apt to call for ten yards. But this may not always be the wisest choice. The defense is counting on the referee's intervention; therefore, they may not be concentrating on a quick transition. A quick diagonal pass that beats the encroacher may be a powerful weapon against this tactic.

This decision should be made by a team captain, someone appointed by the coach to handle such cases. Coaches should teach the other players not to immediately call for ten yards at every opportunity. This only plays into the hands of the defense. While anyone can take the kick, it makes most sense for a defender or midfielder to do so, in order to have target players in front.

Free kicks at midfield can be treated similarly, but perhaps with more intensity and quickness. One pass can put a team in scoring range. The team with the better organization and discipline will win the advantage. To train players for quick transition, the coach must clarify their responsibilities: At the whistle, they must anticipate and react. (The whistle means "GO!") The player nearest the ball retrieves it, and, if necessary, throws it to the player nearest the location of the restart, who has already chosen a target player or space. A stopwatch can be used to time the transition, and motivate players to move quickly. The diagonal pass is usually more effective than a straight forward pass. Forwards should look to get behind the defense. Midfielders can offer support.

In the attacking third, free kicks will have to deal with a wall of a varying number of defenders. This wall almost never allows the full ten yards, even when repositioned by the referee. But even younger players can chip the ball over the wall to an oncoming teammate for a quick shot. Older players may be able to shoot around the wall with a banana kick. Or they may have enough accuracy to put the ball through a hole in the wall. Many defenses are terribly disorganized in wall setting, and do not even respond to the screams of their goalie to move left or right. This lack of organization can be exploited by a properly trained team.

If the defense is well-organized, it may be better to play the ball over or around the wall. Many teams devise set plays for both direct and indirect kicks in the attacking third. These plays are only as good as the techniques of the individual players. The key is to keep it simple, and go with your strengths. If you have a player who can curl the ball around a wall, use him. If your team has a strong header, get another player to chip the ball to him.

The way to open up space in these restarts is to fill in space vacated by a marked player who brings the defender with him. The essential attacking areas are, as always, near post, far post, and center. However, the offsides rule may restrict these possibilities. Therefore, a direct kick on goal may still be the best weapon.

An assessment of the opposing goalie is especially valuable in these plays. Can the keeper reach the corners? Can he move left as well as right? Is the keeper's vision blocked? Does he come off the line readily? This knowledge will help a team to plan a successful strategy on free kicks.

Now let us examine these free kicks from a defensive standpoint. We have already seen how organization, discipline, and quickness play a major role in any defensive situation. Another important aspect of defending against free kicks is thorough knowledge of the rules, coupled with the highest regard for sportsmanship. The professional foul has no place in youth soccer. If coaches insist on clean play and refuse to condone intentional fouls, teams will give up fewer direct kicks. Though perhaps obvious, this concept is too often ignored. Young players should be instilled with the spirit of fair and clean play. Therefore, coaches should spend at least as much time teaching the rules and fair play as they spend organizing defenses against free kicks.

That said, it is recognized that all teams will give up free kicks. Excessive delay by any defender must be discouraged not only for the sake of sportsmanship, but also because a well-coached opponent will exploit this momentary let-down with a quick attack. The mental disposition is extremely important here.

Along with this attitude, young players can benefit from another helpful concept. In special situations it seems that players are invariable coached to DEFEND against a quality ball being delivered toward the goal. Perhaps a better mind set would be to place more emphasis on WINNING the ball, as well as more concern for areas of the field that become uncovered as a result of marking. Ball winning and area coverage is important because scoring chances result from picks and movement into space vacated by a marked man.

Practice against picks, especially those that verge on being illegal obstructions (moving picks), is a necessity. In fact, players must be coached to defend against illegal plays because these are not always noticed by the officials.

The principles of defending against free kicks in the midfield and back third can be readily seen in the previous discussion of the offensive free kick from those areas. But the free kick within scoring range calls for a wall. Members of the wall must have courage, but the best defenders must still be used to mark the most dangerous scorers and the players most able to penetrate. All walls must protect the near post, with at least one player fully beyond the imaginary line from the ball to the near post; this is to defend against curving or banana shots.

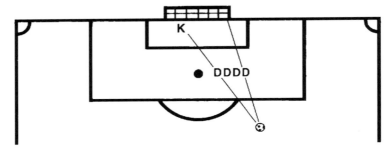

**Diagram #71: Keepers also need to <u>see</u> the ball.**

The number of players in a wall for direct and indirect kicks should generally follow the guidelines illustrated in the diagram below.

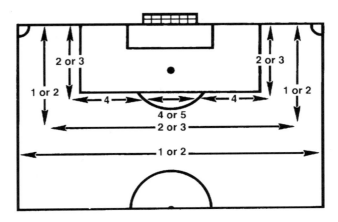

**Diagram #72: These are guidelines. The individual keeper (or wall builder) may call for more people in the wall, esp. against dangerous free kick specialist.**

Who sets the wall? On most youth teams, it is the keeper. But since the keeper has a great deal to attend to in these situations, such as making sure that all attackers are marked, someone else may set the wall. Often it is a striker or wing, who has little other defensive responsibility. Communication between the goalie and the field players is vital. Frequently the free back is the most talented in this regard.

A corner kick is essentially a cross; therefore the attacking principles are those discussed in Chapter VII, which deals with the strike. Let us then focus on defending against the corner kick. Again the mind set of winning the ball and area coverage is essential. Defenders should be conscious of the keeper's voice and style. They must also realize that all balls should be cleared by going forward; if one cannot get the ball by going forward, it belongs to someone behind him or the keeper. All players must certainly understand this concept.

This training must be fully developed, and is best taught by merely setting up in front of the goal, using two groups (a defense and an offense). Through repeated trials, the coach can teach the rules, check for flaws, and assess individual strengths, such as air control, courage, power, and jumping ability. These assets can be used to gain an advantage.

The coach should stress the importance of adequate numbers and correct locations so that defenders can follow the rule of going forward, especially near the far post and central goal area. This requires a minimum of two players, but generally more are required. With enough players in the shaded area of the diagram below, all players can feel comfortable about going forward with conviction.

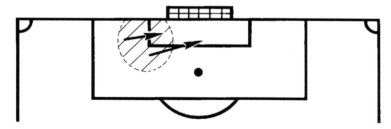

**Diagram #73: Since forward movement is essential, some players should be well beyond the back post as the corner kick is taken.**

Winning the ball depends upon maintaining vision and moving forward with a good power jump. A coaching tip here is to remind players to concentrate on the ball. Defensive headers are aimed higher on the head, the intention being to clear the ball as high, far, and wide as possible. Midfielders and forwards should be trained to anticipate these clearing passes.

The reason for two or more defenders at the far post is to maintain coverage if one of them must vacate the area to track down an attacker. This will allow for defense against the flick-ons to the far post. Another defender is needed to defend against flick-ons to the central area. This defender covers the center of the goal to approximately six yards out. Merely developing an awareness of this danger area in the defensive unit will help to deal with this potent offensive tactic.

During these practices, the keeper must repeatedly decide whether to leave the line to cover the cross, or remain in goal. To perfect the keeper's technique, corner kicks can first be delivered without the pressure of receivers; then other attackers can be introduced to work up to match conditions. A major part of this session is communication. The goalie makes his intentions known with conviction and authority: "Keeper!" or "Away!" Once the decision is made and announced, the keeper must follow through without hesitation.

Like corner kicks, the penalty kick requires special training. For the kicker, it is important to practice under as realistic conditions as possible. The coach can set the stage by by creating a hypothetical scenario: "The score is 1-1 with four minutes to go in a championship game. You are brought down in the penalty area and will take the kick. If you make it, practice is over. If not, everyone does two laps with a ball." (In a real game, the coach should do just the opposite with the penalty kicker; that is, take the pressure off by expressing confidence in the outcome: "Don't worry about the kick! I know we'll achieve all of our goals anyway.")

Kickers need to practice placing the ball towards the corners of the net; goalies will not be able to reach these areas. Accuracy is more important than power. The kicker should pick a spot (the back bar of the goal is frequently excellent) not too close to the corner, and not change her mind at any time from the approach to the follow-through. Psychological games bordering on poor sportsmanship between the kicker and the goalie have no place in youth soccer. Neither should get caught up in them. It is more likely that such poor behavior will backfire; in any case, it does nothing for the game.

This is just as important from the keeper's standpoint. The keeper, however, is not really at a psychological disadvantage: everyone expects the kicker to score, so all the pressure is really on the kicker. Whether the penalty kicker will pick a spot or blast away, the keeper is well advised to simply obey the rule and not move his feet until the ball is kicked. Surprisingly, a good number of both types of kicks (the picked spot and the blast) go to the middle of the goal. The keeper who guesses without any information misses these shots, as well as shots to the opposite side. Therefore, the ever-popular blind guesswork is a poor tactic.

Fortunately, there are clues to help the keeper anticipate the direction of the penalty kick: the approach, the spot where the foot meets the ball, prior knowledge of the kicker's style, better foot, or favorite target. The keeper can consider all this information, but it is where and how the kicker's foot finally meets the ball that tells the most. This ultimate piece of information allows very little time for the keeper to react; nevertheless, proper training can help the goalie improve reaction speed and build confidence. For in-depth information on defending penalty kicks, as well as all basic aspects of goalkeeping, see So Now You Are A Goalkeeper by Joe Machnik and Frans Hoek. Both now have their own video's which are excellent. Again, knowledge of the rules and experience is the best prevention of penalty kicks; defenders must be very aware of the type of contact permitted in the game.

Awareness of the rules and basic principles of soccer and player roles is also critical to the most common restart: the throw-in. Except with very young players, coaches should not overlook throw-in violations in practice. Young players should practice the proper technique until it becomes automatic. The long throw-in to the goal mouth is a great weapon. To increase distance and accuracy, training with the bounceable medicine ball is very helpful. See the appendix article "Use of Medicine Ball in Developing Technique."

The tactical awareness of throw-ins derives from quickness and the principles of player roles in soccer. With the whistle signaling out-of-bounds, there is often a mental let-down. The team that maintains concentration and hustle gains the edge. This frequently results from fitness, but not always.

The thrower is the first attacker, who needs support from a second attacker and mobility from at least one third attacker. Support comes from a player, often a midfielder, who runs across the field toward the touchline. If marked, this player (the second attacker) may first check out and in to get free. Mobility is most often created by a wing (the third attacker) accelerating down the touch line, but not out of throwing range. The throw-in can arc over the wing's head or bounce beside his feet, to be met at speed. The wing may also need to check in, then out. A fullback usually offers deep support, in the event that the other receivers are marked. In the defending third, the keeper can move to the edge of the penalty area to catch a throw-in. Again, the first law of offense (spread out) and the first law of defense (compactness) are in full force.

Having completed the throw, the thrower should move on to the field of play to offer support. The receiver may be shielding the ball from a defender, and need to return it to the thrower. Another option for the thrower when the receiver is marked and facing the thrower is to toss the ball to the receiver's head for a quick return pass to the thrower's feet. A simple hand signal from the receiver sets this play without being seen by the defender.

Defending against throw-ins is aided by sustained concentration, quick transition, knowledge of the thrower's distance, and anticipation. The thrower usually tries for the wing first, since that is potentially the most penetrating move. Double coverage of that wing may be helpful. A defender given the responsibility of marking the thrower can minimize the effectiveness of a quick return pass. A coordinated team defensive effort will usually force the throw-in back towards the thrower's goal. Defending a long throw-in from deep in one's defending third is essentially the same as defending against a corner kick. As always, numerical superiority around the ball is half the battle.

It should be clear that the principles of player roles on attack and defense hold true for special situations like free kicks and throw-ins. The team that gains the advantage is the team that maintains its concentration after the whistle blows, and organizes quickly and correctly. Restarts are a contest of time. The attack tries to penetrate, support, and mobilize faster than the defense can delay, cover, and balance. While most young teams are conditioned to stop and rest at the sound of the whistle, superior teams learn that the whistle means "GO!"

# 11

## *Team Tactics Coaching*

Coaches and fans love discussions of team arrangements and tactics, but these discussions are not productive for teams with poor technique (dribbling, passing/receiving, etc.) and poor tactics (cannot perform well executed 1/2's, takeovers, overlaps, do not spread out on offense, etc.). Until players have the skill and understanding to execute both the principles of player roles and small group tactics, such discussions are meaningless. Players under fourteen usually require more emphasis on technique and small group tactics, which are best taught using shortsided games. Too often, teams fail to develop players and do not achieve long range results when they bypass these necessary developmental stages.

But once a team is ready for this step, team tactics present a whole new challenge for the coach. High school athletes are usually able to benefit from team tactical instruction. This chapter will introduce the major areas of team tactics coaching: team arrangements, player positions, low versus high pressure, guidelines for teaching tactics, and applying tactics to common situations such as the off-side trap.

To begin, it is important to distinguish a team arrangement from a team tactic. While there is some relationship between the two, team tactics go far beyond team arrangements. Significant team tactics include finishing activities, changes of field, maintaining possession, use of width and depth in attack, rapid transition, use of long and short passes, exploiting an opponent's weakness, and so forth.

The choice of a team arrangement, however, can be a starting point for team tactics, as certain formations lend themselves to particular tactics. No single team arrangement is always best. Any arrangement must depend upon the personnel of a given team. The competition, age, field, and many other factors also affect the adaptations used for a certain match. Sometimes a change simply for its own sake is helpful, as it stimulates new thought and alleviates staleness. A coach must be some what openminded to variations best suited to the team's unique personnel. Sensible adjustment and emphasis of a basic system might be wiser than trying to invent a whole new system.

The basic criteria in choosing a formation are to exploit a team's own strengths and minimize its weaknesses. This is admittedly difficult, and calls for thorough knowledge of each player. While there are certain advantages to each arrangement, usually the basic arrangement is maintained and merely adjusted to contend with the opponent. For example, a team may withdraw its left midfielder or wing to mark the opposing right midfielder because he is their creator. The team formation adapts in order to mark that player out of the game.

Due to its balance in numbers over the field, and its simplicity, the 4-3-3 is a good basic system to use as a teaching model. In fact, all other systems can be considered variations of this. The key to the entire midfield movement in the 4-3-3 is to have the keeper and two of the final four behind the ball while one of the final four is delivering the ball to the midfield. The unaccounted member of the final four becomes a midfielder to lend the necessary four man width. This concept carries through to the strikers; one or more midfielders moves up to create support and width in the attack.

With this or any system, the constant objective is to maintain four man width near the ball. It is nearly impossible to have proper ball support and some mobility without at least four players in the general area of the ball. On defense, it is almost impossible to put pressure on the ball, delay, cover, and concentrate with fewer than four players, especially if the attack involves four or more players. The 4-3-3 encourages fluid movement to add the extra player in midfield or up front; therefore it aids in the development of complete players who overlap.  A further advantage of the 4-3-3 involves the development of wing play. **With two wings, the attack is more apt to use the entire width of the field**. Also, midfielders and backs are encouraged to fill in attacking lanes opened up by wings who stay wide. Any and all systems can be excellent - - the 4-3-3 is ONLY favored as a <u>teaching model.</u>

Once the team can use the 4-3-3 to move a ball out of the defensive third, then through midfield to create a strike, it has learned all the basic principles that aid defending and finishing. It remains merely to apply the same principles to different thirds of the field. For example, the principle of pressure on the ball varies greatly from one third of the field to another. A defender with the ball deep in his own third should consider any opponent within five yards as pressure, whereas a striker with the ball in shooting range may not consider a very close marker as pressure. The safety/risk ratio is the basic principle in these examples.

The bulk of instructional time on team tactics, then, uses the 4-3-3 system. Subsequently, variations may be encouraged with more accomplished players. While the differences among systems of play are sometimes exaggerated, <u>all</u> <u>share</u> <u>many</u> <u>common</u> <u>elements</u>. The constant need for four defenders allows for variations only in the number of midfielders and strikers. These adjustments generally revolve around a team's tactic to possess and predominantly use perimeter strikes, or play more direct high pressure and exploit transition and target players .

Systems such as the 4-4-2 resemble the 4-3-3 in the rear, but vary considerably in striking at the goal. Of course, having only two strikers, midfielders and defenders usually overlap more frequently in this system. The 4-4-2 fosters direct attack high pressure, and transition opportunities. There are adequate numbers of players to deliver to the target players up front. Generally, the one furthest forward is a strong player who plays well with his back to the goal, capable of holding the ball, enjoys taking on a defender, and is willing to take risks. The other striker usually has very good passing and supporting skills, with fine anticipation and vision. These roles are interchangeable.

In general, the 4-4-2 is an attempt to increase the pressure, especially at midfield, and thereby win the ball earlier and more frequently for transition shots on goal. Inspite of low numbers up front, it can be quite offensive, but it demands great attacking effort from every player. It favors a direct method to goal, but also allows for frequent drop passes to create the shot and can also be very wing oriented. Midfielders try to create many 1-2 movements with the two strikers. They aid the strike by overlapping, especially on the wings, where space is often available.

It should be pointed out that the more direct attacks favored by the 4-4-2 system lend themselves better to high level teams that are already capable of implementing strikes through wing play. With younger teams, such direct play can quickly deteriorate to kick-and-run with its accompanying lack of patience and improvisation. This can hinder both technical and tactical development.

Other systems such as the 3-4-3, 4-2-4 and 5-3-2 can be explored with quality players above age 15. These systems basically borrow players from one line to fill other slots. Whether they facilitate four man width throughout the field depends more on the individual understanding and hustle of the players.

Though a great deal more can be said about systems of play, at the youth level it is more or less academic. Instructional time with fourteen and under is best safe guarded teaching the 4-3-3; for older and more skilled players, the 4-4-2 can be introduced. More than anything else players must be given many, many touches of the ball and have hundreds of hours of shortsided games.

More important than any system of play is the question of which position each team member should play. Of course, ultimate player development depends upon experience at every position, including goalkeeper. But most players will show a preference for either defender, midfield, or striker. If at all possible, this general preference should be met at least some of the time.

Physical attributes are not the main concern in choosing positions. Certainly, good heading ability, good dribbling, speed, quickness, and anticipation are all useful everywhere on the field. But a striker who misses two shots and stops shooting, or a midfielder who does not support, is of little value.

The determining attributes of where players play is mental. Put eight players in a 4v4 shortsided game, and note the roles played. Natural defenders will hang back, occasionally going forward. Midfielders will move continuously, offering support and cover. Strikers will take on defenders and shoot. Nearly all players will reveal their natural preferences in any short-sided scrimmage.

Requests for left or right side of the field, however, are a bit more complex. It is helpful to ascertain why the player wants the left or right; it is not always a matter of which foot is stronger. Some players want to link up with certain others, because they are good friends, or they complement each other. Timid players may want to play on the far side, away from the coach, bench, or parents. The particular opponent may also be a factor. There are always secondary concerns to being certain players get development from many touches of the ball, regular dribbling instruction, basic understanding smallsided tactics and players roles.

Whatever the case, soccer is a team sport calling for some sacrifices; communication and motivation can go a long way to satisfying most position preferences. Players will more readily try another position if they know that everyone else must do the same. Choice of positions can also be used as a motivator with older players, as a reward for perfect attendance, good attitude, sportsmanship, and so forth.

Frequently, a team's quality players are consumed in striking and defense, while the midfield is filled in with 'leftover' players. This is a mistake. The reverse is just as big a mistake. There should be a balance of capable players, including some in the midfield. Furthermore, placing all the strength up the middle is not always a good tactic. Players who work well in traffic, ball winners, and scrappy type players usually do well up the middle, especially with good defenders in the rear. On the sides, players who are creative or need a little room to dribble can be a great asset.

The conventional wisdom has long been to build a team from the rear, according to skill level and size, with the biggest, least skilled players at the back. Midfielders and wings could be small. Recently, the consideration of skill level and size has given way to mental factors. The best, most confident athlete belongs in goal, but he/she must really want to be a keeper. Patient, disciplined players make the best defenders. All-around players who always manage to get involved become midfielders. Risk-takers of course go up front. Individual players become wings.

No longer do we confuse size and strength. Many small players play strong and many big players do not. Strength is enormously more important than size, though there is some relationship between the two.

Contemporary ideas for team tactics, as presented by Coach Bob Dikranian, involve balancing three player types throughout the field: playmakers, fighters, and players (a combination of the two). Any team needs all three types, more or less balanced throughout the field. This would put a playmaker, a fighter, and a player in each line. Again the concept of mental attributes is emphasized over physical considerations. There is always an attempt to find a 'schemer' to set things up in the midfield.

Having considered systems of play and player positions, the next step deals with defensive style, low pressure versus high pressure. In youth soccer, low pressure instruction comes first in order for players to understand the basics of first, second, and third defender. Low pressure is essentially the principles of first, second, and third defenders applied to the defending half or third of the field. Since cover is an essential ingredient in defense, and since high pressure greatly reduces cover, it can mislead young players about all the basics of defense. This can lead to mindless kick and run. In addition, very high pressure can lead to strict man-to-man defense, with little regard for zonal areas or the location of the ball. This is dangerous because the ball, man, and area are all vital to quality defense and/or zonal concepts.

To make low pressure work, the concept of getting numbers behind the ball needs to be taught to even the youngest players; however, this must be accomplished by getting back, never by simply staying back.

With its emphasis on zonal coverage, low pressure defense concerns itself with positioning in regard to the vital area. Generally, this system tries to free the final defender from marking responsibilities, so that he/she can offer cover wherever necessary.

While low pressure can save energy for attack, it may lead to low scoring defensive minded games. Some players find it difficult, when playing low pressure, to launch a quick counterattack. These players may be lulled into a physically and mentally lazy game. The antidote is coaching! Skill and self-expression should be encouraged, and immediate movement whenever the ball is lost is a must. Constant motion does not require constant running. **Changes in speed, both individually and as a team, mark a higher level of play**.

These changes of pace are just as necessary in high pressure defense. Another characteristic common to both defensive styles is the need for strikers to immediately chase when they lose the ball. Tackling is also part of both styles. Frequently, great defenders do very little tackling; instead they stay on their feet to protect the space behind them and continue defending. However, all players must know how and when to tackle.

Once the team is firmly able to conduct low pressure defense, it is time to begin high pressure instruction. This non ball touching oriented instruction should last no more than fifteen minutes per session. Where FIFA laws allow for only two substitutes, it is nearly impossible to play high pressure for a whole match. It may be tactically naive as well, if the opponent gets accustomed to it.

High pressure is characterized by tight man-to-man marking, sometimes of every field player. By restricting time and space and denying all support, high pressure tries to force the opponent into errors. All players try to cut out the pass and launch a quick counterattack. When high pressure is successful, it can cause an opponent to lose control of time, space, and the ball. This forces long 50/50 balls out of the final third.

When unsuccessful, this system causes the team applying pressure to waste energy, stifle its own skill, and ruin self expression. Therefore, against a highly skilled and well-organized team, high pressure may be unproductive. High level soccer is characterized by the ability to employ both styles, even in a single match. Usually, the opposing team dictates whether high or low pressure should be used. Sooner or later, situations which call for one of these styles will come up.

Though neither style is superior to the other, players fourteen and older should be able to play both ways. In the modern game high level teams frequently play a combination system which goes thusly: As soon as we lose the ball we play very high pressure to regain it. Sometimes this only lasts for 2 to 5 seconds. Once the team realizes possession is clearly lost the team falls back to play defense. Obviously this is a combination of very high pressure mixed with low pressure.

Developing team tactics that exploit particular strengths or defuse an opponent's attack calls for analysis and creativity on the part of the coach. Beginning coaches should not underestimate the importance of common sense in this area. For example, if the opponent has only one player capable of scoring, that player might be marked out of the game or even double teamed when necessary. Possibly he can be stopped by carefully marking the player who delivers him the ball. It is impossible to treat all the likely situations in regards to tactics. Instead, it may prove helpful to present basic teaching principles to get the team to perform any tactic.

The prerequisites are twofold: First, a team needs players who are faithful in attendance and attention so that they can implement teamwork. For a team that practices twice or more a week, twelve of the usual sixteen player roster should attend regularly. Second, these players must have the maturity, both athletically and emotionally, to execute skills, player roles, and small group tactics, and to respond to coaching. Players under thirteen years usually lack the technique and maturity to learn team tactics. Even many older players have great technical skills, but cannot adjust them to the situation.

In presenting team tactics, the coach must have a very clear understanding not only of the tactic, but also of the various ramifications of the opposition's response to it. The coach must know why she is using a given tactic; then she will also know when and against whom the tactic should be used.

Most importantly, the tactic should be introduced at a practice session, not a match. Team tactics succeed only if the all-important progression works up to match conditions with pressure from equal or better opposition. Many coaches know this process, yet attempt to take short cuts. The mere telling of a tactic does not work; it almost never wins a match that would not have been won anyway. Shouting out unrehearsed tactical instructions during a match is counterproductive. Players need to be prepared for such situations during practice. Otherwise, they realize that the coach has been caught unprepared, and any shouting and negative behavior only diminishes the coach's credibility.

Since many players are motivated by the coach rather than by themselves, serious damage may be done to their desire to play, learn, and improve.They often think that they themselves, not the tactic, has failed. This brings them to the conclusion that their best effort is not good enough for the coach. Coaches introducing a new tactic at a practice session should model the instruction in this sequence:

**Step 1.** Brief (less than five minutes) explanation of the tactic with the use of a clear, simple diagram. This explanation should not be connected to another discussion period or topic.

**Step 2.** A field demonstration or walk through with techniques such as shadow play, 11v0, etc., followed by execution against token pressure that gradually builds up to full opposition. If the marked field was not available for initial instruction, the tactic must then be moved onto the field location(s) where it occurs. If the entire team is involved, maybe you can build from 4 or 5 to 8 or 9 and end with 11. Also, start with a step that precedes the tactic, and try to finish with a step beyond the tactic. For example, in developing midfield changes, start with the backs delivering the ball, and finish with a striker shooting on goal. If possible develop components of the tactic so that players aren't standing around wasting time.

**Step 3.** Experimentation with the tactic in a non-emotional match, such as a scrimmage is important so that stoppages and explanation can take place to review the functions and details of the tactic. For tactics not involving the whole team a shortsided game may suffice.

**Step 4.** A simple and clear handout is given to all players for review. This helps absentees catch up and permits players to discuss the tactic among themselves or ask questions of the coach. Teams that meet daily and that can constantly review items covered may not need a handout.

**Step 5.** Use of the tactic in a match. Generally, the first time a new tactic is used, there is a need for further correction or refinement.

Even with the proper introduction and development of team tactics, a team may find that a given tactic is not successful in a particular match. In this case the coach must ascertain the reason(s) for this failure. Is the tactic being executed correctly? Does the team lack the speed, aggression, or technique to carry out the tactic? How is the opponent beating the tactic? The answers must be made known, or the players may lose faith in a sound tactic that may not be working simply because the opponent is too strong. Even the best-prepared tactics of many world-class teams cannot immobilize a Romario. Thus, generally wins and loses are mostly a reflection of the quality of players on a given team.

With this understanding of teaching tactics, let us now look at typical match situations where tactics can be employed. Our earlier discussion of systems of play should give a team a clue as to the opponent's game plan. A 4-4-2 may indicate that the midfield needs reinforcement, that there are no natural wingers, or that the twin strikers are a real threat. A 4-3-3 may or may not tell us much. More useful is the opponent's defensive style; therefore let us begin with tactics that are designed to counteract low pressure defense through each third of the field.

If the opponent plays low pressure, its defense will withdraw and take its stand in its own half or third. This leaves the back third open, allowing the final four on the attacking team time and space to work the ball forward. These players should be particularly alert to exploit any laziness by the retreating defenders. There may be no pressure on the ball as the final four carry it; therefore any one of them may have time to deliver a quality ball to a strategic location. These players should be taught to look for a free player, an area where their teammates outnumber the opponents, and also for a teammate making a run to space. In general, if the attacking team does not use the time and space it is given (in other words interpassing among themselves while still looking for a good opening), it has allowed the low pressure defense to have its way.

In the event that the opposing strikers do chase back and

put pressure on the ball, the final four must maintain numbers up. Composure is most important here; because strikers are often fast and aggressive, they may cause the final four to panic. The coach must teach them to deal with this through practice. Generally, strikers, even those who are adept at defense, are weak defenders. The very attributes of a striker, such as risk-taking, can be a liability on defense. Their tendency to overcommit on defense can be exploited by players who remain unshaken under pressure. In short, defenders with dribbling, shielding, and passing skills can often get past the first line of defense without risk.

At midfield, a fast dribbling attack at stationary defenders is often a successful tactic against low pressure defense. Combinational play which is initiated by dribbling fullbacks can create excellent opportunities. This can lead to an overload in one area.

As penetration reaches the attacking third, the defenders must react. But if the attacking team has the momentum, it can move the ball more quickly than the defense can organize. A penetrating dribble, a quick 1-2, or a cross can exploit a defense's slowness. The penalty area may be crowded with defenders. If the attack merely 'dumps the ball in', it will probably lose it to the more numerous defenders. To upset this packed-in defense, changes of field are effective. As the defense shifts to cover the new point of attack, it may open up space for a penetrating pass and shot. Such packed-in defenses are vulnerable to fouls, handballs, deflections, and blocking the keeper's vision. Attackers who shoot low and early are most likely to catch the defense disorganized. A team should practice these against a packed defense, perhaps building up to a 11v12 (or even 6v8) scrimmage where the team of 12 stays in its own half of the field.

Once a team can adjust its tactics to counteract low pressure defense, it is ready to deal with high pressure. Against high pressure, the final four will be marked when they have the ball. If they have numbers up, they should be able to handle themselves, as long as they do not panic. With numbers down or equal, the long kick from the keeper or a back becomes a useful tactic. Long, accurate passes can take a number of defenders out of the play. Numbers down in the back third means numbers up at midfield or the attacking third; therefore a long pass can be devastating. Any 5v5, 4v4, or 3v3 which leads to a 1v1 is worth the chance. Small group tactics can create such a chance.

These tactics should be practiced so that the final four maintains its composure and delivers an accurate penetrating pass. Opposing forwards often shepherd the backs toward the touchline; this may permit a penetrating pass to the wing. The final four can then move up quickly to support, and catch the opponent off-sides if the ball is lost.

Ultimately, the team that recognizes and adapts to both low pressure and high pressure defense has a great advantage. This ability to play slow and fast, and to change pace quickly, must be developed in practice if it is to work in a game. It is important to learn to switch from slow to fast, and from fast to slow. Low pressure can provide the energy for quality high pressure.

Overemphasis on any one style, whether on attack or defense, is not top class. No team can reach its potential by playing every day with the same strategy. Today's game demands versatility, the ability to play both low risk and long ball attack, as well as low pressure and high pressure defense. The choices depend first on a team's personnel, conditioning, and natural style, and secondly, on the opponent. Other factors include field size and condition, weather, time remaining, and especially the score.

One tactic bears special consideration here; that is, the off-side trap. In youth soccer, the inability of players to process all the information necessary for the off-side trap must be recognized. While some teams under fourteen have used the trap effectively, this is true only because the attacking team has not practiced tactics against it. It is actually easier to teach tactics for breaking the trap than it is to teach the trap itself. With proper training, beating the offside trap is quite simple. For the coach, setting a mental framework that an off-side trap is easy to beat is the first step. Of course, players must clearly understand the rule; walk-through demonstrations maybe are necessary.

To beat the trap, the central striker must push all the way up to the final defender. A constantly moving striker may force this defender to concentrate on marking more than on calling the trap. Passes, usually chips, can be sent over the defender; if the striker is faster and positioned ball-side, it is simply a matter of timing and communication. Even equal speed is frequently adequate because the striker is facing the run and the defender is facing the wrong direction. Diagonal passes are usually more effective; they keep the striker on-sides more readily, and allow him the space advantage. Long balls to the corner flags are useful with fast strikers. Diagonal runs are obviously safer than straight forward movement. When combined, so that two attackers cross each other, these diagonal runs have the added advantage of confusing the defense.

Dribbling beats the off-side trap. A player cannot be called off-sides for dribbling the ball through the defense. Therefore a good dribbler is a major weapon against the trap. The advantage here is that beating one defender usually beats all of them, as the trap forces defenders to be flat and play without cover.

Another successful tactic is the overlap from one or more midfielders or backs, who are often left unmarked. These players may beat a defender with a dribble, or pass the ball to an unmarked supporting player. Using 1-2 movements with target players here or at any time will not only beat the trap, but catch the defense moving the wrong way. At the edge of the penalty area, exchanges are a great tactic; when well executed, they can result in a quick opening for a shot. Maybe the most devastating tactic is for <u>forwards</u> <u>to</u> <u>withdraw</u> and have midfielders move forward.

Tactical work requires thorough understanding, preparation, and patience on the part of the coach. From team arrangements and positions, to defensive and attacking style, to considerations of one's strengths and weaknesses, as well as the opponent and many other variables, team tactics require time and attention. For skilled players who understand and implemement the principles of attack and defense, tactical training will yield very positive results for a team and satisfaction for the coach. Team tactics with young players are never conducted with sacrifices to ball contact, player development, or shortsided work.

The next chapter will offer tactics to help the coach maximize training time and effectiveness.

# 12

## *Shortsided League Games and Indoor Training*

Anyone who has seen a full field game among beginning players under the age of twelve can bear witness to the chaos which results. Even novice adults who find themselves on the field with twenty-one other players experience a great deal of confusion. Does it have to be this way? The answer is no! The fact that adult soccer uses eleven players on a hundred yard field does not mean that this arrangement is also best for inexperienced players under twelve years of age. Coaches and program directors should also consider the fact that no country in the world recommends 11 aside for players under twelve! We have already proven the benefits of shortsided games as part of practice sessions. This chapter will present a strong case for shortsided league games and indoor training that hasten the technical and tactical development of young players.

Actually, 11v11 for youth under twelve would be comparable to 18v18 for adults. The confusion, compaction, and contact can only be imagined. To make the comparison in the other direction, 6v6 for youth is like 11v11 for adults. This is due to relative skill and strength levels. Young players do not strike the ball far and accurately enough to contribute positively to a full field game.

Shortsided league play is preferred to 11v11 games for many reasons. Players can only improve through abundant practice with the ball. In a 90 minute professional match, each player actually has contact with the ball for less than two minutes. Young children do not possess the ball as well, and have shorter games; therefore, they get very little ball experience in full-size games. Consequently, they have less involvement, and less fun. This leads to less running off the ball (less support), probably the fundamental element of developing quality soccer at any age. Six aside matches essentially provide twice as much ball experience as full-sided games.

Shortsided games present better opportunities to be open to receive a pass. Therefore, players tend to go to open space with the realization that they may get the ball. Passing becomes more frequent and purposeful. Increased support raises the level of play above the chaotic bee swarm. This opens the possibility for more use of space and increased vision, which lays the foundation for short passing. Altogether, 6v6 offers appropriate space, skill, power, and time to implement a game that truly resembles soccer.

Skill development is thus enhanced by shortsided games much more than by full-sided games. One technical example is a major aspect of dribbling; namely, feinting. In its early stages, feinting must work in order for players to want to develop it. In the bee swarm, feinting is meaningless, for there are players immediately nearby in every direction! In 6v6 there is space to allow an attacker to beat an opponent with a feint.

Another example is tackling. In 11v11 with young kids, tackling is of little use. If a player makes a clean skillful tackle, the ball will probably go to another player in the pack. Young players then begin to substitute kicking away at each other for proper tackling. Technique gives way to mindless blasting away at the ball.

What about scoring? Generally, the number of goals scored relates more to the number of people defending a goal rather than the number attacking. Smaller sides allow for more (and possibly better) goals, which multiplies the fun and excitement for young players. Smallsided games are free to use keepers or not. Obviously, with keepers, larger goals are used.

Positional play is greatly reduced in shortsided games. This allows players to develop all-around soccer skills rather than only one aspect of the game. This eliminates the misplaced emphasis on functional training with very young players. With players moving around more freely, the games begin to resemble quality soccer. Everyone must mark at times, and help each other. Teamwork advances rapidly. There is far less standing around.

In shortsided games, the principles governing first, second, and third attackers and defenders come clearly into play. This is the very foundation of tactical awareness. With this understanding, defenders will tend to compact and attackers will spread out, intelligently applying the primary tactic of higher levels of the game. Once this is established, transitions from attack to defense, and vice versa, become simpler, quicker, and more efficient.

There are even administrative advantages to shortsided leagues. Two six aside games can be played simultaneously on a full soccer field. In fact, the full soccer field with goals is no longer necessary. This eases scheduling problems, and frees up field space, which is at a premium in many areas. A single referee can maintain better control with fewer players and less space. The need for experienced referees is decreased, and more people might become referees since the job becomes easier and less intimidating on the smaller field. One coach or parent could easily handle the substitutions for both games. In fact, if one person were to coach both games simultaneously, it would at least diminish the amount of yelling and negative behavior from the coach. Players would be allowed to let the game become their teacher.

The case for six aside league games could be further supported, citing nearly every aspect of the game. In many countries, shortsided league games serve as the transition from street soccer to full-sided matches, which can occur somewhere around the age of eleven. In America, where street soccer has not yet taken hold, the need for six aside is even more pressing. Sound development of the game depends upon shortsided programs.

As soccer grows, more and more shortsided leagues are springing up. Six vs. six need not be rigid. Some places prefer 4 aside for ages 5-7 and eight aside for ages 8-11. Even organizations which insist on full-sided games for their very young players recognize the value of smaller sides when they establish indoor programs during the off-season. Maintaining skills during the winter, at least in northern climates, requires indoor training. These programs are generally six aside, not by design, but rather by the space limitations of typical gymnasiums. Nevertheless, they offer most of the advantages of an outdoor six aside experience, including conditioning, technical development (especially in close quarters), decision-making, and tactical awareness.

There are some great advantages to training indoors. The surface is smooth, dry, and level. The ball rolls and bounces more predictably and precisely on a gym floor. Wind, rain, and darkness are not a problem. The change of pace indoors can be stimulating and refreshing. Skill can play a greater role than aggression or power, if we promote it.

In addition to these advantages, there are of course some differences. While not necessarily disadvantages, they may change the nature of the game. The outdoor game calls for sophisticated pacing, whereas the frequent substitutions of the indoor game encourage all-out effort for short periods of time. This can be used as interval training, a very good conditioner for the outdoor game. In terms of tactics, the long ball is virtually eliminated; intermediate and short passes, 1-2 movements, exchanges, and combinational play become the tactical choices. The emphasis is on the greatest possible accuracy and precision.

Also the demand to change roles quickly and completely is greater in the indoor game. Defenders must be able to strike and shoot. When they do, the need for a striker to move into a defensive role is imperative. In short, the indoor experience is excellent for development of 'total soccer'.

We must not overlook the value of the indoor game for shooting. The reduced height and width of the goal calls for greater accuracy and consideration of angles. While the low ball that is not on goal frequently rebounds to permit another opportunity, the high shot is wasted. Indoor players soon learn that keeping the ball down is a good idea. Even so, the chip shot is still a great indoor weapon, as it can be used to keep the goalie from coming out too much to deny shots.

Indoor training presents an excellent opportunity to improve individual techniques. Frequently, during the season the need for tactical development and team coordination leaves little time for players to build individual technique. Advanced dribbling training can be a focus of these indoor workouts. Stepovers, chops, sole rolls, lifts, and power drives can be done in order to beat a single opponent. Special attention should be given to feints, shields, and 1v1 activities.

Much of the appeal of indoor training stems from indoor tournaments and professional indoor leagues. This creates enthusiasm and offers models for young players to emulate. There are two distinct sets of indoor rules, however, each bear discussion because they affect player development. A look at the MISL (Major Indoor Soccer League) will give us some background. During the 1970's, when the MISL was in its infancy, the indoor experience was essentially soccer played indoors, very fast in pace, with exciting displays of individual skills and spectacular goalie saves. With the wide use of rebounds off the walls, the action was virtually non-stop. Players depended greatly upon fitness and technical skill. With the ball and players moving and changing directions at such speed, tactical organization was low on the scale of importance. This is quite typical of any game at an early stage in its development.

Much has changed since those early years. Through the middle 80's even the least successful team in the MISL began to show definite signs of advanced tactics in both defense and attack. Definite styles of attack have evolved and clear organization now exists for man up situations that occur spontaneously, as well as those that result from the 'power play'. Crisp ground passing has increased enormously. Most importantly, there is less use of the boards, and when the boards are used, there appears to be more purpose.

This brief history points out the direction of the indoor game's development. Although fans, especially the uninitiated, may enjoy the non-stop action of the ball bouncing off the boards, some research indicates the less the boards are used, the higher the level of soccer.

This realization gives rise to another type of game, which is known as 'mini-soccer', or Futsal which uses a low bounce ball. Mini-soccer does not use the walls; there is an out-of-bounds. Many coaches find that mini-soccer is a great variation of the indoor game. Because this game can be played in unsophisticated facilities, its use as a training method is growing. But the major reason for recommending this form is that it demands and develops playing the ball with control and purpose at all times.

One proponent of the mini version, Anson Dorrance of the University of North Carolina, agrees: "There is no question that mini-soccer is technically the superior form of indoor soccer. Use of walls encourages sloppy technique. When you have a sideline to negotiate, you have to be precise in where you pass the ball, how you take it down the court, and how you beat opponents in tight spaces."

The final plus for the mini-soccer version is that it is an international game, thereby inviting additional experiences. One might add that FIFA has taken a look closely at both forms of indoor soccer. Indeed there is room for both varieties, especially in terms of player development. As a result they have created the five aside game which is a combination of the two games. It has no walls, but it uses a live ball. While all are valid, the deciding factors should be the facility, age and ability of the players. Very young players may benefit from the continuous flow that walls provide; this would give them more contact with the ball. With older players, however, using the walls may hinder their technical and tactical development. Certainly the wall is not an evil in itself; the misuse or overuse of it, however, does present a problem.

For reasonably skilled athletes playing with walls, then, it is wise to limit the use of the walls only for getting the ball to an intended receiver at a specific location; in other words, only for 'wall passes.' Blind use of the boards only hinders player development in terms of intention when releasing the ball. This misuse could become a major setback for young players, who need a great deal of time and quality coaching to develop constructive ball habits.

All three games contribute to rapid and close collecting, 1-2 movements, quick thinking, and quick, accurate shooting. All teach a great deal about rapid transitions and require players to attack and defend more urgently. Strikers must defend more and defenders must attack more. This develops complete players.

In summation, both types of indoor soccer can be valid forms of the smallsided soccer which is so vital in total player development. However, the use of walls presents some important cautions. The indoor game is a new phenomenon and is in a period of rapid growth. The United States of

America is very much a part of this growth, and this interest in shortsided soccer and indoor training will advance our development of the great outdoor game, which is examined further in the next chapter.

# 13

## *Continuing Growth in Developing Soccer In the United States*

While good coaches develop their players as people and athletes, they also develop themselves as role models and teachers. Each season they seek to improve their craft. While continuing to observe matches, attend clinics, read articles, and watch videos, they also learn from their own meditation. Though this description may depict a professional coach, it also applies to the part-time volunteer coach who seeks excellence. Each year, the youth coach may get to only a few college or pro games, or clinics, or read only one book. But making a child's soccer experience a positive one requires knowledge as well as love. The coach who shows his studiousness in regard to the game provides a better model.

While guidance from informed sources is important, the personal reflections of the coach should not be underestimated. Such consideration allows the coach to solve specific problems, which often relate to communication and motivation. Frequently, the coach knows the player, the family, the community, and the program better than anyone else. No soccer 'expert' knows the particular group as well as the coach does. Combining the coach's own contemplation with outside resources creates a role model that will be respected and remembered for a lifetime. If this could be turned into a formula for the successful youth coach, it might look like this:

| Knowledge + | Concern + | Meditation = | Quality Coach |
|---|---|---|---|
| (many sources including administration) | (love) | (realizing one's importance & uniqueness) | (positive lifetime memories) |

The role model image is the single most important feature. Respect, morality, manners, controlled language, even appropriate attire all contribute to a quality role model. A clear set of values and an approach to discipline, while unique to each individual, are also essential. The quest for improvement is easily sensed and appreciated by kids. They need to know that we all continue to learn, and must learn, in order to grow.

Again, the criteria for excellence have little to do with wins and losses. A commitment to fun, participation, and emotional and athletic development reflect a coach who feels that both the players and the game are important. With this attitude, the coach will not only grow in the activity, but also derive greater enjoyment. This provides a role model whose behavior conveys the message: "It's hard work, but it's worth doing!"

To deal with the work load, coaches need assistants to handle the various duties, such as communication, information, equipment, meetings, transportation, and special training sessions. Parental involvement alleviates problems and helps build for success. Administrative ability also allows the coach to concentrate on coaching, a prerequisite for the success of a team or program. Anson Dorrance, former National Women's coach, places administration second to no other aspect of coaching in order to enjoy team success.

These enlightened approaches are beginning to make inroads virtually everywhere in American youth soccer. More coaches are becoming sensitive to a child's needs; more coaches are becoming aware of how we learn; more coaches with playing experience are bringing more knowledge to their teams. The National Youth Sports Coaches Association is training and licensing thousands of coaches every year. The United States Soccer Federation and the National Soccer Coaches Association of America have both created new advanced courses that focus on youth soccer. More parents are sharing their children's enthusiasm for the great game. The game continues to grow, change, and become more competitive. The game of ethics is now American. At this moment, we are on the brink of becoming an adolescent soccer nation! The World Cup Tournament, which was only a dream a decade ago, was our sounding success in 1994.

A World Cup trophy, only a dream now, will one day follow. Due to our large population, cultural and climatic variety, wealth, history of accomplishments, and most of all, our great athletes, success is inevitable when we become a mature soccer nation.

Still, the pessimists fear the extinction of soccer and point toward the lack of a professional league. The fact remains, however, that the NFL took well over fifty years to establish itself, only after repeated failures. Others decry low scores, ignoring the fact that today's young players will patronize a game that they love and understand. The informed appreciate the entire game, seeing goals as a bonus for creative passing and dribbling. They understand goal mouth chaos, great collections, powerful shots, athletic saves, accurate heading, turning from pressure, etc. It is safe to predict that it will be more difficult to arrest a professional soccer league in the future than it is to establish one at present. In the meantime, our better college teams can serve as role models as well as MLS giving youngsters hope of a career in playing professionally.

But a professional league is only one aspect of developing the sport. The game will advance when it can draw from a large pool of 'hungry' players, likely to come from less affluent economic classes. Street soccer, therefore, is imperative to our improvement as a soccer nation. Basketball players were never produced at UCLA, as John Wooden is quick to express; they are self-developed in cities on cement courts with less than ideal conditions. As the great game reaches further into the inner city, mental toughness will reach new levels. The player for whom there is no alternative to success plays on against seemingly impossible odds.

Affluent America's form of street soccer, backyard soccer, will also contribute. With millions of boys and girls playing soccer in the cities, suburbs, and countryside, the talent pool deepens. The growing number of leagues and youth tournaments will bring players from every social strata together on the soccer field.

Of course, we may be several decades away from this point, but we must first realize where we want to go if we are to get there. It is not too much to say that we want to go where baseball, football, basketball and hockey are, where boys and girls play their games in streets and backyards long before they join organized teams; where kids flock to professional games and read about their heroes in every issue of Sports Illustrated.

This is not to say that we want to replace any of these sports. Such a notion is absurd. Apple pie has not disappeared, even after hundreds of additions to the American diet. Pizza, tacos, strudel, hamburgers and hot dogs coexist, as will soccer and other sports. Any attempt to suppress the game will only make it stronger. The United States will likely be a five major team sport nation instead of four. History bears this out: once we were a one sport nation, then two, then three and possibly someday it could be six.

But how do we get there? We can begin by looking at other countries, then adapting this information to our unique situation. The entire body of experts recognizes street soccer, visible heroes, a strong positively unified national organization for players, quality officiating, and capable sports medicine as the key elements of soccer success in any country, including the United States.   The need for street soccer continues to be vital. But along with this, we need to step up the promotion of the game in the inner city, for there is virtually no major network exposure and far too little cooperation with nearby suburban programs. Television provides visible heroes that give young urban athletes the inspiration to excel; suburban leagues give them the opportunity to play on good fields with decent equipment and organized coaching. The athletic ability of the urban athlete could then combine with the organizational ability of the suburban program.

Of course, there is a need for a strong national body to organize the various sections, ages, and levels of the game. The USSF has proven itself capable of winning the trust of the soccer world and FIFA by landing the responsibility of the World Cup. This event has showcased our talent for organization and promotion; if we can do this for the whole world, we can certainly do it for our own country. With the most sophisticated communication, information and media networks in the world, we certainly should be able to promote our sport. Quality officiating, which can only evolve from more experience and selection than is now possible, will be a natural consequence of soccer's growth in the next few decades. Officials who have played the game bring a wealth of knowledge and experience, which can only improve their performance and everyone's enjoyment of the game.

Also, training and sports medicine for soccer must reach the same advanced levels that it has in other American sports. At present it is only average, but as more sports medicine personnel deal with soccer training and injuries, the level of understanding will naturally improve. The increasing knowledge of the specifics of soccer will lead to a better understanding of the special stresses that the game puts on the player. Our outstanding equipment for general fitness and athletics will help bring training methods to state-of-the-art.

One aspect of training that Americans can not afford to ignore deals with the unlimited substitution permitted in most American soccer. At the youth level, this helps to develop the bench and often results in victories. Even when this is not the case, all must play. The coaches who lament their lack of bench strength are usually the ones who have not developed their substitutes. Even the notion of a sub or second string is antithetical to youth sports; everyone should get to be a starter some of the time. Furthermore, players should be allowed to play full uninterrupted halves instead of being shuffled in and out of games.

But free substitution at the advanced level may cause some problems. It tempts a team to play constant high pressure; this creates players who are mentally impoverished to play a whole match. Due to free substitution, possibly the greatest deficiency in United States soccer is in the midfield. A quality midfielder who is not replaced develops a keen sense of pacing, while those who are substituted invariably lack this important skill. Those players with olympic, professional, or world class ability must learn to play whole games in order to pace themselves properly for high level tactics, skills, and the varied rhythms of the game.

Lastly, there must be an evolution in soccer coaching, particularly at the youth level. As players become coaches, there will be a natural elevation to a higher stage of development. Player coaches develop thinking, especially in the area of purposeful passing, which is difficult to achieve without player experience. The most important coaching advance will have to be in the understanding of player development. Presently, most soccer coaches know what elements of the game to teach, some know how to teach these elements, but few know when to teach these various elements. Proper development depends upon the right step at the right time, based upon sound principles of physical and emotional growth. This book is an attempt to elucidate these steps.

This development of players in America most emphatically begins with street and backyard soccer as the very young players' introduction to the sport. The emphasis is on fun, ball control, and attacking skills; technique and tactics are developed simultaneously. With this background, the child's first league experience should be shortsided, stressing player roles in attack as the foundation for small group tactics. Then by age eleven or twelve, these players would be more capable of the full-field game, continually increasing technical and decision-making skills, as well as introducing player roles in defense. At age fifteen and beyond, functional training could begin to help players build on their strengths and minimize their weaknesses at particular positions.

Within this framework, there is still room for a variety of coaching techniques and styles. Soccer has the great advantage of drawing from a worldwide body of knowledge. We can learn a great deal from information, systems, styles, and coaches of countries with forty or more years of high level international experience with accompanying professional leagues. On the other hand, to ignore these sources is to reinvent the wheel. Also, it is perverse to profess a body of knowledge gathered from only one source, whether one expert or one nation. Generally, by copying one nation, coaches are limiting growth. Even recently migrated coaches must learn from countries other than their own. Because our climate, culture, fields, player mentality and attributes, and coaching are somewhat different, the answer is not to copy Italy, Argentina, Germany, England, Holland, or any other single nation. We need people who are truly international in their knowledge.

This could be an American or a foreigner. In any case, it

must be someone who is willing both to study the world game and to recognize our total cultural milieu, our physicality, mentality, disposition, problem-solving, values, and creativity. We do not need foreigners trying to implant their country's system in the United States; nor do we need Americans who are ignorant of the world game. Only from this global view, which is another way of saying from this philosophy, can we maximize our success.

All successful soccer powers learn from each other. Therefore, we must understand all the various systems and styles. Only then can we build an original system based upon our own players, and therefore best suited for us. The most successful team styles seem to evolve from the uniqueness of the players and coaches.

With that in mind, can we describe how the American system might evolve? While somewhat speculative, it is worth considering. First of all, it is probable that our system will be very **versatile**. With our literacy, intellect, and temperament, our players will master a well-rounded repertoire of soccer skills and tactics. As street soccer spreads, there will be no deficiency in **individual skill**. Add to this our extreme **coachability**, admired by many visiting coaches from all over the world, and we have the markings of extraordinarily **versatile teams**.

Our diverse climates and ethnic backgrounds also affect a variety of styles. And our athletes play many sports in which **tempo changes** are common, like basketball, football, hockey, and tennis. Thus they will be able to change speed and play both high and low pressure. Our leaning will be toward **high pressure** because of our moderately cool climate, quantity of athletes, their collective temperament, and physical attributes.

Due to American football and culture, there will be some tendency to be quite **physical**. This must be used constructively, not at the expense of skills and tactics. The emphasis must be on honest courage for 50/50 balls as opposed to playing the man. Our **size**, **strength**, and **speed** will enable us to exploit the air ball.

The abundant use of hands in other sports should carry over into soccer. The **throw-in will be a major weapon of**

**penetration**, not just a way to get the ball back into play. Of course, there are also implications for keepers. Americans' excellent hand strength and coordination, combined with our **great size and courage, will help produce many great keepers**. Our weakness at this position will probably stem from our notorious **lack of patience**.

Our large population would seem to assure uniform strength in all positions, with **great depth** on the bench. While enormous geography tends to limit us, our affluence will help to overcome this. Our lack of proximity to any country except Mexico and Canada hampers much international experience, but our wealth permits long trips. American players as young as ten years are travelling all over the globe for soccer experience. However, our high level international experience with players in Europe is escalating rapidly.

**Overall, contending teams from America will be fast, versatile, tending toward high pressure, excellent at one touch passing, able to control and exploit the air game, and anchored by excellent keepers. Eventually, we will develop coaching techniques which rank with the most advanced in the world**.

This book has been an attempt to introduce some of these techniques. It stresses fun, participation, and development over winning. It focuses on integrating technical and tactical development as the necessary foundation for functional training. It supports a bias toward street soccer and smallsided games. It clarifies and applies the principles of player roles to all aspects of the game. It emphasizes attack over defense, decision-making over drill, and developing players over collecting trophies. And it elucidates what to teach, as well as how and when to teach. While not a complete guide, this book does represent a complete approach, where knowledge and love of the child combine with knowledge and love of the great game of soccer.

All responses are welcomed and I hope this book has inspired many to learning even more about *The Great Game*.

# *Appendix i*
# *The Prepared Coach*

This appendix item focuses on equipment and how to use it. The philosophical preparation of the coach has been discussed in previous chapters. The actual business of coaching also entails a mental plan, which includes a long range plan for a season or even a few years, a short range plan which could involve a single session, and perhaps even an intermediate plan for a week or two. While the long range plan may be more general, the daily plan enumerates specific activities to achieve a specific goal.

Therefore, for each practice session, a clearly defined written plan is a must. For a single session it may be just a 3x5 card, as long as each activity is clear in the coach's mind. A Soccer Practice Planner is highly recommended, as it organizes a whole season according to sound principles of player development and effective practice. In this practice planner, a coach can keep attendance records, a seasonal team plan, individual objectives and progress, and daily practice plans.

Once a coach has a plan and a safe playing area, it is time to obtain the necessary equipment. The tools of the soccer trade are relatively inexpensive, but there is the usual range of quality and price.

Ironically enough, one of the most important ingredients for a safe and effective practice or game is practically free, yet often neglected: WATER! As Dr. Bob Burns points out, a player can lose as much as two liters of water per hour. Such a rapid fluid loss can reduce the blood volume to the muscles which need it most. The result can be loss of drive and concentration, often cramps in healthy athletes are rarely caused by low levels of potassium, salt, calcium, or magnesium.

The amount of salt that they lose during a regular match should cause no harmful effects, such as cramps; but dehydration can. If dehydration is allowed to occur, neither salt tablets, oranges, nor bananas will eliminate or prevent cramps. Children on balanced diets should have ample electrolytes, minerals, and vitamins to make it through soccer games, only needing water.

Players must replace their fluids. The fluid should not have high concentrations of sugar or salt. Concentrations of 2.5% or less are fine. There should also be water available during the game when a player needs to quickly replace fluids. The water should be cool, and players should be encouraged to drink it even before they feel thirsty. The sensation of thirst can come along after the actual need for fluids. Allow plenty of water breaks, especially during hot weather.

The coach or assistant should have several balls for practice, but in many cases with youth teams, it is best to require players to bring their own ball. This ensures that each player has a ball, encourages touches of the ball before and after the training session, and allows for a warm-up if the coach is detained. It also removes a burden for the coach who has other items to carry. The coach should have several balls for those players who have forgotten, or came from a place other than home.

These soccer balls carried by the coach should be the same as those used in matches. At least on their home ground, players should be using a ball which they used in shortsided or scrimmage activity during training sessions. There are situations where balls are given special treatment for specific reasons. For example, they may be under inflated for heading activities, or over inflated to simulate a match which will be played on hard ground. A pump and needle are therefore necessary.

The prepared coach also has an adequate medical kit, including a first aid guide. Other necessities include large gauze, ointments, and tape. Coldpacks are not as good as ice, but should be included for occasions when ice is not available. The kit should at least suffice until a trainer, ambulance corps, paramedic, or physician can take over. All emergency contact numbers should be available, perhaps on the outside of the kit. Extra shoe laces can be kept in the kit. If eye glare is part of the kit, it should be used in a practice session to help the player safely adjust to it. Avoid introducing new elements at a time when there is match excitement.

For shortsided and scrimmage activities, scrimmage vests are needed to ensure clarity. Otherwise players have to go shirts and skins or light colors against dark. A child who is overweight, underweight, has a scar or any abnormality may be very reluctant to take off or change a shirt. The coach should not press this issue. Scrimmage vests help to avoid such situations.

A whistle and some sort of coaching board for explanations can also be included. For players fifteen and older who require conditioning work, a necessary tool is a stopwatch for taking pulse rates. Players should learn how to take their own pulse. After conditioning work, players should count their pulse for thirty seconds, then multiply by two for the actual rate. Fitness levels require a rate over 150, but for more mature players, serious fitness requires even higher heart rates. A good training session will get the heart beat to this range several times in a light session and possible ten to twelve times in sessions that emphasize fitness. Double check with a doctor.

Some type of markers are needed; they may be cones, disks, corner flags (or obstacle course markers). These can be used to lay out grids, small fields, goals, and obstacle courses. Of course, these areas would ideally be lined out with a field marker, but portable markers allow more flexibility. For dribbling and accurate passing practice, obstacle course markers are very useful. They can also serve as small goals. Though they may stick out of an equipment bag somewhat, their lightness and versatility make them a very functional tool.

A single container or equipment bag allows the parent volunteer to quickly prepare for practice, thus making the job easier, more efficient, and more fun. On game days, an extra game shirt of each color is in order. As virtually all play requires shinguards for every player, extra guards become necessary. Home games require corner flags, nets, net fasteners, pegs, and team benches. A scorebook should be kept beginning about the time players reach the age of fifteen.

If one is predisposed in this direction, it can begin much earlier, but careful use should be made of it. It should not be used as a discussion piece. While a scorebook can reveal much information to help in choosing and designing training activities, it is not usually helpful to share this information directly with the players.

Since shooting should be part of every practice, goals are necessary. Practice goals should be the same size as match goals. These should be down-sized for players under twelve. Attackers should practice shooting at goals with nets. The time spent putting the nets up and taking them down is made up by not having to retrieve so many shots. Nets also give the attacker a more visible target. Net pegs are an often overlooked item; some teams weave a chain through the bottom of their nets to hold them down.

For safety, enjoyment, economy and versatility, goals of all sizes must be portable; that is, able to be easily carried by two to four people. On fields with permanent goals, the goal mouth is invariably bare. Without turf, players' falls are more serious, keepers' dives are more dangerous, and play becomes unpredictable, causing more collisions and injuries. With unpredictable bounces, tactics and strategy break down. Chance replaces control and skill. Added to these safety and enjoyment factors, the economy of portable goals becomes obvious when consideration is given to the high financial and time cost of repairing turf. Injuries and lawsuits decrease when goals can be moved to safer areas. Portability not only allows for different size playing areas, but also for different goal configurations, such as sideways, back-to back, or diagonally, depending on the objective of the exercises.

Full-size portable goals must be lightweight, but to resist vandalism, they must also be very strong and impossible to disassemble if they are to stay at the field. Other goals which are taken home should be easy to put together, take apart, and fit in a car. In any case, portable goals are a must in an era of multi-field usage.

Goal size is important! A full-size goal for younger players rewards bad shooting habits and technique, while punishing good keeping habits and technique! This is absurd. Goal size must be appropriate in terms of the field-size, the size and number of players, and whether there is a keeper. But a different size goal for each two year age group is impractical. Many programs do not have enough enrollment, fields, or funds to justify so many different size goals. Many state associations are adopting 7' x 21' goals, which the United States Youth Soccer Association Playing Rules suggest for players between eight and ten. This may still be too large for younger players.

Therefore a compromise is in order, but this compromise should be based on the same two concepts that determine adult size goals: goals must be low enough to be defended, and wide enough to encourage decision-making and good foot movement. This reasoning would call for two youth-size goals. For ages 5-7, a goal size of 5' x 15'; for ages 8-11, a goal size approximately 6 1/2' X 18 1/2'. These goals have significant width, with reduced height so that keepers can truly defend the goal. Players age twelve and up would use full size goals, since nearly all keepers in this age range can reach within 4" of the crossbar.

To this equipment, other items can be added, depending on the age and gender of the team. Training balls of all sizes, medicine balls, pendulum header balls, target nets, rebound nets, two-sided goals, indoor goals, field markers, rule books, water bottles, goalie gloves and pads, and referee equipment can all contribute to the enjoyment, efficiency, safety and success of a program.

# Appendix ii
# Finishing Activities
# Using the Two-Sided Goal

Training with two-sided or flat-faced goals has been recommended by Wiel Coerver and Franz van Balkom, and used with great success in Holland. These are lightweight portable goals approximately 7' x 20' which can be assembled in two minutes or less, and easily carried by one person and moved by two people after assembled. They are free standing, allowing use of both sides simultaneously. When the net is tied taut, the ball hits it, stops, and drops in front. When the net is loosely tied, it takes the pace off a low shot, then lets the ball roll through safely to a player on the receiving side. This versatility allows for continuous motion and circular drills, and adds conditioning to shooting drills. Padded floor shoes can convert the goals for indoor use.

In general, these goals permit more than three times the number of shots as a traditional goal in the same amount of time. With two usable sides, waiting in lines is no longer necessary. With flat nets, the time lost retrieving balls "buried" in the net is totally eliminated, as is the need for net pegs. The safety hazard of someone being struck by a ball while retrieving is also eliminated.

The slightly reduced size promotes accuracy and eliminates the wasteful practice of using a keeper as a ball retriever. There is no unnecessary destruction of the keeper's confidence, since he/she is not placed in front of a net where nearly all balls will score. Virtually all shooting activities are aimed under the colored rope which runs parallel to the ground at a height of four feet. Targets can be attached to the corners for further accuracy.

Quality finishing requires repeated trials at a full-size goal. Once shooting is technically sound, pressure is added, then players build up to shortsided games with specific restrictions. Using a pair of these goals, immediate transition and counterattack can occur after each score. The following is a series of finishing activities using one, two, three, or four flat-faced goals.

**Takeover and Shot**

Activity one: (Net tied tight for balls dropping after contact.) Player A dribbles and leaves the ball for player B who takes the ball and shoots, with A taking the follow-up shot as the ball rebounds off the net. Player A retrieves the ball and dribbles to the starting point, then passes to player B. The process is repeated up to ten times, then the drill can begin from a different angle or the opposite side. Adjust and vary distance according to ability of players; first occasion might be from 12-15 yards away. Two other players can practice this drill on the other side of the goal. See diagram.

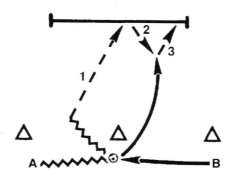

**Diagram #74: Takeover creating a shot on goal.**

Variations can include different shooting techniques, one touch shots, two touch shots, change of direction before shot, fake takeover exchange, one touch heel pass, chips, and headers.

## Wall Pass and Shot

A and B attack Goal II. Player A dribbles with eye contact preceding a pass to Player B. Player B waits for the right moment, makes bent run and accelerates to reception of the ball. Both players follow the shot.

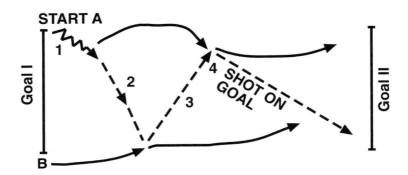

**Diagram #75: Wall pass emphasizing quality.**

Three pairs of two players may be ideal. The other side of both goals can be used for other activities.

## Through Ball and Shot

Player A dribbles, player B calls for the ball with an accelerated run. Player A chips the ball to space in front of B who controls the ball with ANY part of the body, and hits a forceful low shot to the far post. If a one touch shot is possible, all the better. Emphasize low shots, well under the four foot marker rope on the goal.

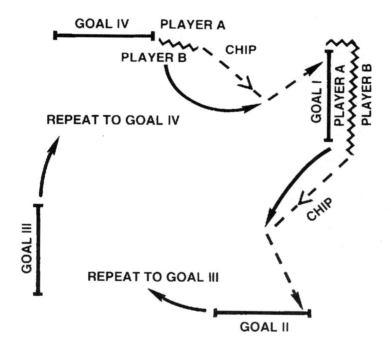

**Diagram #76: Players never seem to be bored when asked to shoot at goal. This activity involves serious fitness as well.**

From two to twenty players can easily be accommodated. With fewer numbers, this can be turned into a form of interval training. Both players follow the shot and run around the goal posts before they exchange roles and go to the next goal.

## Crossing and Heading

With O2 dribbling, the three attackers start at Goal II and move toward Goal I. O3 makes a bent run to the near post, and O1 makes a bent run to the near post. O2 delivers a well-timed ball to either post: a hard-driven ball to O3, or a lofted ball to O1. The receiver heads the ball into the goal. Another group can repeat the drill to Goal II. Practice from either side, then introduce defensive pressure (one to three players).

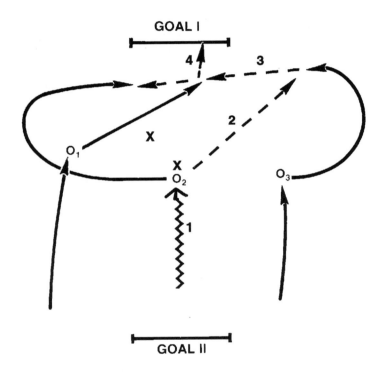

**Diagram #77: Heading goals are very exciting, but only will be achieved with reasonable regularity by training.**

## Volley Shot:

Player A on one side of the net, serves over the net to player B, who aims a full volley shot low at the net. With the net tied loosely, the shot will roll through slowly, coming to rest at the server's feet.

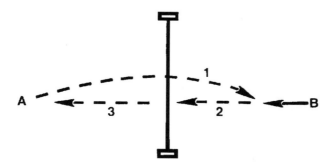

**Diagram #78: The ability to shoot volley shots help goal scoring a great deal.**

Options include a half volley; receiving the ball with the body on full run then shooting on second touch; heading shots; two receivers, one setting up the other for a perfect shot; addition of keeper for passing shots (under twelve years old).

This is how the net works when tied loosely.

## Long Passing and Shot

As shown in the diagram, these circular activities provide innumerable repetitions of a skill in a short period of time. Again the net ties are set loose so that the ball comes through the net with no retrieval necessary. It is good for developing accurate long passes with four players.

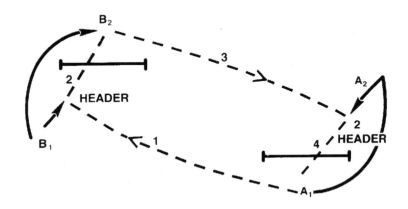

**Diagram #79: This provides excellent practice for serving as well as heading.**

Options for this activity include chipped balls to central goal area (away from keeper); 90° ground balls (move goals slightly for varied angles); driven balls to near post; driven balls to the chest; and using two receivers, one to flick the ball on to the other for a shot.

These goals can also be used for many keeper activities, such as punting at the other side of each net, throw-ins to a target on the net, or diving practice saves of kicked balls, etc. The array of activities is limited only by the coach's creativity. For more ideas, see the Budweiser tapes by Franz van Balkom.

**These goals have limitless uses. The only limitation is the coaches imagination, and judging from what many American coaches have suggested to me, our U.S. coaches are enormously creative.**

# Appendix iii
# Using the Medicine Ball in
# Developing Technique

Unlike the standard dead weight medicine ball, the Kwik Goal Soccer Medicine Ball has life (bounce) which makes it useful for many exercises and drills. It is used by more than 10 National team keepers throughout the world. Many activities done with a regular ball are improved with the medicine ball. Field players can use it to improve distance and accuracy of throw-ins, while goalkeepers can use it to develop many basic techniques. For example, the 'pull back' movement (as in baseball catching) is facilitated due to the weighted ball.

The ball's two-pound weight develops power more than strength. The regulation size and thirty-two panels allow for a realistic grip. It is durable and marked for safety, as it should not be kicked nor headed. Throw-in activities are wonderful drills in the U.S. because they allow us to build on our good use of the hands. Using the medicine ball for throw-ins develops distance, which in turn helps accuracy, since the thrower is no longer struggling to make the throw. The receiver gains possession more quickly.

A proper program for use of the medicine ball is essentially the same for all power work. Players throw the medicine ball 6-12 repetitions, then throw a regulation ball 6-12 repetitions. Repeat this cycle 3 to 5 times (set). Using this program every other day (three times a week), for four to six weeks will greatly improve distance.

For goalkeeper training, the ball's ability to bounce overcomes the limits of working with a traditional medicine ball.

While the bulk of a keeper's work should involve decision-making, the medicine ball is best suited for technical training. Some medicine ball activity can be done in season or out, outdoors, or in a gym, basement, or living room.

Essential goalkeeper attributes such as agility, mobility, and footwork all begin with flexibility; its weight slows down the movements so that each muscle must work more fully through its range. Here are some FLEXIBILITY exercises using the medicine ball:

### 1. Two-Handed Bounce/Catch

Keeper stands with feet facing one direction, bounces ball and catches it, using hands and body lift to cushion catch. Without moving feet from original position, ball is bounced in front of player, on side of player, and behind player going 360°. This activity is also good for abdominal flexibility.

### 2. Overall Flexibility

Lying on back while holding medicine ball between the feet, the keeper slowly lifts legs overhead to achieve maximum safe stretch (not to point of pain). The ball helps the neck, back, trunk, and legs to stretch. This can be done side to side as well as forward and backward.

### 3. Flexibility and Ball Handling

These activities can be done alone or with a partner. Alone, the keeper rolls the ball on the ground in figure eight patterns through the legs, then bounces the ball through the legs in various ways, such as front to back, back to front, and sideways. In pairs, keepers can pass the ball through legs, then around, then overhead and sideways. These activities can be incorporated into warm-up and stretching. There are numerous variations, including side to side passing and side to side figure eights.

Another area of keeper technique is QUICKNESS AND FOOTWORK. Here are some suggestions for developing these important qualities using the medicine ball.

### 1. Quickness of Reflexes and Catching

Keeper faces wall a few yards away. A server behind the keeper throws ball over keeper's head at wall; keeper must react quickly to make the catch. Pulling hands back with the weighted ball develops proper technique.

## 2. Footwork

Two servers alternate serves to each post. Keeper saves the ball at one post, returns it to server, and immediately uses side to side shuffle to save ball at other post. Steps must be small enough to maintain balance and allow for quick change of direction. After initial stage, serves can be at random, so that the keeper must change direction quickly.

Of course, any sound program of catching and throwing activity using the medicine ball will dramatically increase STRENGTH. But for developing pure hand strength, try this idea.

### 1. Strength Development

Working in pairs, each player tries to wrestle the ball away from the other. Using hands only builds a better grip of the ball. Many different starting positions can be used, such as lying, kneeling, and sitting.

In the area of CATCHING SKILL, the medicine ball emphasizes several important techniques. Try the following progression.

### 1. Developing 'W' Catching Skill

Modern keeping demands a partial closing of the 'W' so that four fingers as well as thumbs are behind the ball. This is sometimes called 'O' catching. Fingertip catching and quietness are emphasized. Catching the "top half of the ball" is stressed. Begin with ground ball catches with proper form, then sideways catches of low balls.

### 2. Diving Saves

In the diving progression, the weight of the ball helps to carry the keeper through the proper motion, according to leading keeper trainer Tony DiCicco. Emphasis is on lifting the hips so that hands are free to make saves low, away and high. The medicine ball provides a quality cushion.

Another technical area is MULTIPLE SAVES. The pace and intensity of these exercises can be adjusted, with frequent breaks for technical training and rapid succession for fitness training.

### 1. High/Low Multiple Saves

Server alternates high and low balls for keeper. Emphasize quickness and the proper mental disposition of constant effort until ball is safely in keeper's hands. Do at least three rapid repetitions. Variations include emphasizing one area, dives, and recovering from a dive.

For improving DISTRIBUTION technique, the medicine ball can be thrown or rolled to targets, improving accuracy, then distance. The keeper throws at a target, keeping score of the number of hits. When the target is hit ten times in a row, increase the distance.

See Bibliography for Medicine Ball Book by Tony DiCiccio.

# Appendix iv
# A Plan for a Soccer Training Complex

This facility could service any club, camp, school, college, or professional team. It would be especially helpful as a training center for USSF and NSCAA courses, Pan Am Games, state and Olympic development programs. A quality training facility requires many stations for individual work, diagnostic work, grid training, diversified shooting experiences, strength, conditioning, and most of all, team tactics.

Besides teaching quality soccer techniques, such a complex provides fun, organization, and great economy of training. Furthermore, all the equipment for the entire complex would only cost approximately $5,000. Much could be accomplished with even $3,000.

**Area I** is an inclined speed running area (3 to 5 degree maximum), modeled after Russian inclined speed running techniques to improve cerebral processing, lengthen stride, and give muscles the sensation of high speed. Down hill speed running on the modest incline is an important activity for speed development. Though plyometrics is probably number one, bungy pulling can also be significant.

**Area II** is an angled kicking board and pitchback for receiving and turning high balls at innumerable angles both left and right. Balls are accurately delivered to the pitchback and power driven onto the kicking board.

**Area III** contains Dutch gates or grid gates used for lifting body weight, especially for fitness. These can be used to force a body weight jump and simultaneously head the ball. Passing-receiving acceleration runs can also be done in this area.

**Area IV** is a series of pendulum headers. For young players, this is used to practice technique; for older players it can also increase the vertical jump for the air game. In addition to jumping, goalies can use this facility to improve punching, tipping, and timing.

**Area V** is an obstacle course, which is used for dribbling practice. Suggested activities include using one foot, using a specific part of the foot, feinting at each flag, practicing specific moves such as scissors and stepovers, and accelerating at each flag.

**Area VI** is a grid field, used for hundreds of activities, from 1v1 up to 6v6, including shielding, turns, 1-2 movements, first and second defender responsibilities and distances, and recognizing when 3v2 becomes 2v1. A major point of emphasis here should be activities that culminate with a specific type of shot, working toward quality finishing.

**Area VII** contains two-sided goals that allow immediate re-use of the ball without retrieval. This is good for developing intensified shooting and low, accurate shots with head or foot. The goals can easily be arranged in any configuration, so that specific activities such as chip shots can be efficiently practiced. Soccer volleyball can also be played here.

**Area VIII** is a full-sized target net which may be used from both directions. This provides economical shooting practice, since the target rebounds the ball to the player. Targets can be moved anywhere on the goal net face.

**Area IX** is a keeper training area, where sand pits reduce the initial fear of diving, so that technique can be developed faster. The soft landing permits numerous repetitions of forward and lateral dives with proper landing.

**Area X** is, of course, the main field, which is relieved of much wear and tear by using the other areas for specific training activities. Two sets of reduced size goals can be placed on the touchlines, transforming the full field into two small fields for six aside games.

Thus, in an area roughly the size of two soccer fields, a complete training complex can be installed, providing fun and economical training with a minimum of turf damage to any one area. The motivation alone that such a facility can provide for a team or league is well worth the investment.

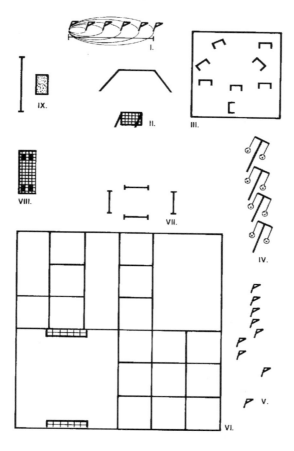

### SOCCER TRAINING COMPLEX

| | |
|---|---|
| I | Inclined Speed Running Area |
| II | Kicking Board and Pitchback |
| III | Dutch Gates |
| IV | Pendulum Headers |
| V | Obstacle Course Area |
| VI | Grid Field Area |
| VII | Coerver Goals (Shooting) |
| | Also: Soccer Volleyball Etc. |
| VIII | Target Net |
| IX | Keeper Diving Pits |
| | Net Wall Behind Pits |

This type of area provides specificity and economy of training. It is great for camps and to provide 'breaks' in regular routine training. See bibliography for developing a multi field complex.

# *Appendix V*
# *Suggestions for a Typical*
# *Effective Practice*
# *Youth Coaches Guide*

For high school varsity and above the steps are similar, but usually only II or III is performed and more time given to Step V.

An effective practice teaches a basic technique, tactic or concept and then masters it through several stages of development. It starts with simple activities without pressure and ends in a more complex activity with pressure. There should be regular changes of activity throughout practice. The following five steps should serve as a guide for the various segments of the practice.

    I.      Warming-up & Stretching  (10-15 min.)
    II.    Individual Technique and/or Tactics (15 min.)
    III.   Group Tactics (small sided games) (45-55 min.)
    IV.   Special Situations (Restarts) (5-10 min.)
    V.    Team Tactics, Scrimmage, more Shortsided game (5-15 min.)

Remember to have special activities for the keeper.

The individual technique (Roman Numeral II) that is taught is the focus of the entire session and is evident in every part of the practice.

# I.WARM-UP AND STRETCHING(10- 20 minutes)
## A.Warm-Ups.

Generally use the ball—while stretching is static, warm-up is movement-oriented including running, dribbling, juggling, and passing. The idea of warm-up is to get an abundant flow of blood through the muscles of the body. This is done by increasing the pulse rate. When the heart is pumping faster and harder, the muscles will get 'warmed'-up. The stretching activities will increase the athletes flexibility. Stretching cold muscles can actually break down muscle tissue and restrict flexibility. Warm-up exercises may include:

1. Youth teams should always include a minimum of 10 minutes of dribbling moves. Most days the dribbling is 20 minutes or more, but the minimum of 10 minutes is a must. Generally every player has a ball, but some of the dribbling activities can be pairs with partners, facing each other, then dribble toward your partner, then changing direction when a yard away from each other.

2. Have two lines, 10 yards apart, facing each other (if more than 11 players present, set up 2 groups) that carry on ball exchange activities. In this activity players can dribble and leave, pass two touch, one touch, dummy, touch-feint-pass, chip, head ball, collect from air serves, etc.

3. Juggling, lifts and drops are still great warm-up activities contrary to opinions versed by some. However, players must move (walk), change directions, use both the left and right side of the body, go from low (foot) to high (head) parts of the body and must drop the ball for a collection. Relifting the ball should be done in a variety of ways. In short, juggling is good when it does not use repetition of the same body part in a boring manner, but when used as prescribed here it is an excellent warm-up activity. To increase the flexibility aspects of juggling emphasize the outside and inside of the foot as this stretches the leg and abdominal muscles beautifully. Finally, have player 'catch' (collect) the ball with various body parts.

4. Circle Activities: passing, one or two balls, add one or two defenders, leave your spot and go where you passed

it, or a vacant cone, wait until defender commits, and other ball exchange activities.

5. Groups of 2 or 3 players: collecting, dribbling, shielding, passing, heading, playing keep away.

6. A grid 20 yards x 20 yards with pairs passing; when near someone go slow and possess; in the open drive (dribble fast); release ball to partner when partner calls for ball which is done by accelerating (running fast). Be certain eye contact is made before the pass.

7. Shortsided exercises, 3 on 3 shooting at small goals (or use corner flags, obstacle course markers, grid goals).

8. Dribble in a grid and follow coach's commands - - lift ball, feint, inside the foot, outside the foot, turn, scissor, chop, etc; emphasize looking up and speed adjustment (near someone, keep ball close; in open space drive fast).

9. Games such as soccer volley ball or soccer tennis may be included here. Catching games are excellent . You can run without the ball, but not with the ball. This is done with 2 teams playing keep away.

10. Some days warm-ups should include passing and receiving activities such as 4v2. Another good warm-up is short long passing with 3 players; the long pass is always supported by player who did not deliver the long ball. Dribbling, feints, exchanges, 2 touch passes, are all included by the two players who are close to each other. The long ball is sent one touch and it is passed on to the player who supports with one touch. This tends toward combination play. This of course begins to set a high level mentality which is tactically upsetting to any defense.

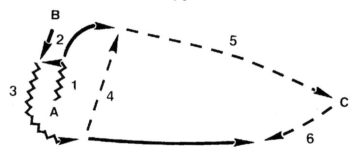

Passes 5 and 6 are both one touch passes in order to encourage combinational movement of ball for the match. Movements 1, 2 & 3 are dribbling or passes involving, 2 or more touches and emphasize accuracy.

At some point the keeper and final defenders separate to warm-up together in order to improve communications, build confidences and for carry over to the days of competition.

The keeper should have vigorous receptions (fly, rolling and bouncing balls, long throws, volley kicks and dives). The keeper should have the possibility of 100% success in the balls that are given to him on the days of games so that he not only warms up his body but his confidence is built and thereby he is mentally ready for the contest.

**All practice transitions should be quick and smooth.**
**B. Stretching.**

The warm-up has provided blood circulation necessary to proper stretching. Often stretching is incomplete because some basic muscle groups are not stretched. Stretch muscles of all seven basic muscle areas:

1) Neck Area - side to side, forward to back. Overcome hand pressure of self, or teammate. NEVER omit neck area since the occurrence of injuries in this area can be catastrophic. Neck exercises are for strengthening as opposed to increasing the range of motion. Recent studies discourage forceful stretching of the neck area.

2) Upper and Lower Back - forward, backward and side ways.

3) Abdominals - often neglected but widely used in soccer.

4) Groin Area

5) Upper Leg - front and back (thigh and esp. hamstring)

6) Lower Leg - calf and side (esp. achilles)

7) Ankles and Arches - ankles rotated; arches by standing on toes for approximately 10 seconds.

Use static stretching (a slow controlled movement) as opposed to any ballistics (jerky, bouncy movements). Basically once the muscle is felt, back off slightly, and hold for a period of time. Generally three to five repetitions of approximately 15 seconds or more are adequate.

The colder the weather or the older the player, the longer the stretching time.

General suggestions regarding stretching:

Use Variety of Procedures - sometimes individually and other times in pairs, usually with ball. Younger groups and/or early in the season stretch together, later on with older groups it can become an independent activity.

Stretching should be accompanied by humor, questions, cues regarding previous or future games, etc. INTERMINGLED warming-up & stretching is excellent. Good blood flow is maintained for maximum stretching.

## II. INDIVIDUAL TECHNIQUES AND TACTICS

Whatever technique is chosen to be done in this segment, becomes the focus of the entire practice. However, space, time and pressure are manipulated and activities move from individual to group to a team situation.

A. Possible skills to be taught: dribbling, passing, collecting heading, shooting, shielding, tackling, and ball turning. Tactics might be square passes, actual runs, overloads, etc. However, you must be very specific. Instead of passing, make it outside the foot passes preceded by a feint, or low trajectory power instep shooting, or volley clearing.

   1 ) Specificity is important to clarify details. For instance, a volley shot on goal received from the wing almost seems to defy basics because the kicker has non-kicking foot off the ground, leans forward and away from the ball, contacts the top half of the ball hip-high. Without the correct details the whole skill is almost impossible to execute. Always attempt to INTEGRATE a given technique to a given tactic. Ex. outside of the foot pass combined to 1-2 movement that involves proper acceleration to receive.

   2) See if you can break the technique down to its main parts and demonstrate the various segments. An advanced player can often demonstrate while the coach explains it. Correction will be easier if you can identify segments of the technique. Of course the

whole skill must also be seen. Give a clear picture for the player. Only correct practice makes perfect! If someone makes good progress on a particular technique have them demonstrate. Accentuate the positive. "That's a good steady head", "excellent follow through", "I can see improvement, the crowd will love the goal you score with that power", "good control," etc. Correction is a must, but the preponderance of 'COACH TALK' IS POSITIVE. Continue a skill by adding pressure (less space or time, or more active defenders). Some days individual tactics are substituted for technique. All sessions have shortsided games to put to use whatever was taught.

3) Keeper Instruction. Example: Accentuate proper knee bend and hand reception of ground balls. Do not forget the keeper in your planning.

4) The keeper's learning must also be put into a game like situation involving decision-making and/or practicing the technique learned in a match situation.

## III. GROUP TACTICS

Observe the individual technique taught in 3 v 3 or similar situation. (4 v 4, 4 v 3, 4 v 2, or whatever GROUP situation is suited to the skill taught.) Generally the 3 v 3 is preferred because of the simplicity and increased ball contact. Therefore, a greater amount of practice is achieved in a given amount of time. A simple clue for beginning coaches is that if only one ball is in use for more than a 1/2 hour of practice you probably could have had a better practice. Keep the idea of stations, small groups, more than one ball, more than one activity (ex. keeper doing dives, field players do 3 v 3 with emphasis on feints), and positive reinforcement. Remember, you can always make it succeed—if it's not working, reduce the pressure, add space, give more time, make it simpler, or do only part of what you intended. If you're feeling frustrated or angry or find yourself yelling, consider giving more space and time or less pressure. If the skill is altered and permits success, everyone will be happier and learn more.

Sometimes it is necessary to completely change the activity and come back to it in a future practice.

## IV. SPECIAL SITUATIONS

Special situations are kept to a minimum for young (under 12) players.

Special situations are preferred before scrimmage (team tactics) because it MUST NOT be forgotten (omitted) in view of the fact many goals are scored from restart situations. Be certain to practice all transitions: goal kick, corner, indirect, direct, penalty kicks, drop balls, and throw-ins. Include shoot-outs if used in your league. Practice quick transitions from defense to offense, or O to D. Be sure to do much of this practice in relation to goal with your regular keeper in net.

Appropriate keeper instruction should be given for various special situations.

Create make-believe situations and then practice for that situation. Pretend there is a 30 mile per hour headwind or crosswind, a muddy field, poor field surface, opponent is in great condition, opposing keeper moves out too much, great sweeper, or whatever your most formidable opponents do. Coach calls out: "We are in Denmark for the World Youth Title with 40,000 people present and you have a penalty shot. Go ahead, shoot!"

## V. TEAM TACTICS

Scrimmage need not be 11v11 full field with keepers. In some cases 8v6 or even 6v4 or even 5 on 5 is adequate. We will only consider 5 basic positions: Strikers, Midfielders, Fullbacks, Free back and Keeper. Anytime we have the strikers supported by midfielders attacking the final defenders (full backs and free back) and the keeper, this is team tactics. This is practical since many coaches have no more players than this to work with at any given practice.

Possible activities: establishing a spread on offensive possession, establishing width on an attack, lateral runs, wall passes (1-2 movement), through balls, midfield shooting, final defender overlaps, etc. Other possibilities include what various players (strikers, midfielders, final defenders) should be doing on offense and defense in each third of the field. The emphasis is still on the technique or concept taught that session.

Any drill worth doing is worth doing several times,

repeating drills avoids wasting time on instructions (and other talk) and keeps players in movement and contact with the ball. Every practice cannot be the major teaching of something new, but one major idea a week is reasonable. Encourage watching games in the community, on TV, attendance at pro games, etc. The coach, if present, may want to ask players questions while watching or point out special features of the games. Do not talk continuously.

The keeper can generally go in goal for the team tactics part of a practice. Note that alternating of high aerobic activities with less active activities. Players must be forced to remain active for reasonable periods and then recover.

| PRACTICE STAGES | Young Players | H.S. Players |
|---|---|---|
| | (Approximate Time) | |
| I. Warm-Up & Stretching | 10 minutes | 15 minutes |
| II. Individual Technique | 15 minutes | 15 minutes |
| III. Group Tactics (shortsided games) | 55 minutes | 45 minutes |
| IV. Special Situations | 5 minutes | 10 minutes |
| V. Team Tactics (6 v 4 or more) | 5 minutes | 15 minutes |
| (Scrimmage or 11 v 11 with keepers) | | |

Players ages 5-10 essentially only do Stages I-III.

Transitions must be smooth and quick.

With youth teams EVERY practice involves player development. This generally means dribbling instruction in addition to other basic player development aspects such as passing and receiving, shooting, etc. Yes, there may be 20-30 minutes of a 1 1/2 hour session devoted to preparing for a specific opponent who has a specific tactic. However, player development must exist in every practice and for the majority of the practice. This is true simply because the role of the youth coach is development, fun, and sportsmanship, not trophies and wins. Of course, we play every match to win, but not sacrificing development, fun and sportsmanship.

The second reason we always put the priority on development is because youth teams frequently are not capable of team tactics due to lack of technique and lack of understanding of small group tactics.
Example: a keeper should kick long when the other team stays forward; but most of the time he should release to his

defenders because most of the time his opponents withdraw to midfield and therefore, have numerical advantage at midfield and beyond.

The problem with youth teams is that they frequently DO NOT withdraw, so the long ball would be appropriate. On the other hand many keepers cannot reach the midfield line or beyond.

In any case, development precedes team tactics. Many team tactics are near impossible due to lack of technique, lack of small group tactics and undeveloped discipline. At the very least it would take up more time than its value and would thereby diminish player development.

## SOCCER PRACTICE GENERALIZATIONS

- Try to use progression which starts with the simple and moves to the complex. A carefully developed sequence GREATLY helps player development.
- It's best to have a thread of continuity for the entire practice—relate all activities for the session to one skill, or at least relate several parts of the practice together.
- Have a ball available for every player (players can bring their own; coach backs this up by also bringing some balls).
- Every practice should involve shooting at goal with some form of pressure.
- Always have a goal available and a net on it so that good habits are developed (i.e., players shoot at corners instead of at keeper).
- At times use stations.
- At least part of the time divide into smaller groups.
- Attempt to have players with the ball as much as possible
- Never omit the thinking parts of the game (establishing width, etc.)
- Instead of coach talk, design a drill that teaches what you want players to learn.
- The idealized five part practice is obviously not always possible, but at least change activities regularly.
- Have scrimmage vests, cones, obstacle course markers, soccer balls, medicine balls, pendulum balls and first aid

kit, etc. available.  It might take a year or two to obtain all the **equipment**, but BEGIN.) The entire team needs to contribute rather than the coach being financially burdened alone.  Just as team work is necessary on the field financial matters require a fair share from everyone.

- ALWAYS HAVE A COMPLETE PLAN, even if you deviate or change it—(you can never get to where you are going unless you have an idea where you would like to go).
- Most people function best with a written plan; use practice planners for yearly and daily plans.
- Advance planning of the practice is vital.
- BE POSITIVE.
- ASK QUESTIONS instead of constantly giving answers.
- **Economical coaching** (one drill which incorporates a given technique, group & team tactic and/or conditioning) is a must.
- Always have water at the field.
- If you only like games and **not practices**, consider coaching a different sport.
- **Players should enjoy practice**, but just as important the coach should enjoy the practice too.
- You are a **role model**, a leader, and have much more influence than you may realize. Try to find something positive in every practice for every player, ESPECIALLY the weakest players—with your confidence in them, they will gain confidence and therefore play better.
- Work with **everyone** at various times (not just the group, but the individual). Try to have 5 or 10 minutes at every practice devoted to 1 or 2 players. Be fair, alternate who you work with at each practice.
- Try to have one contest, game, or **fun activity** in every practice and think mostly of rewards. Not another part to the practice, but one of the five EXISTING parts might fill this need.
- Constantly encourage players to **practice on their own**; juggle, play 1 v 1, 2 v 2, shooting, kicking at a wall, hang a ball from the tree to practice heading, work out with small balls (3", 4 1/2" and 6" balls are great for this purpose many great players are developed from small ball

activities; note, the Brazilians).
- Move all grid activities to **working on goal**.

## SOCCER BASICS.
- When in **possession** all players must think, act, support and be offensive; when the other team has possession, everyone is on defense.
- Offense usually wants to **spread out**, that is, use full width of the field and have depth, though overloads often take place at the same time.
- Defenses should want some **compactness**, cover, and pressure on the ball. On any change of possession, these behaviors should be immediately visible (spreading out or compactness).
- A player spends better than 95% of the game time without the ball; learn to **be useful without the ball** (dummy runs, etc.).
- Call for the ball by **accelerating to a receiving position** (generally open space) and checking <u>to</u> the ball).
- Help your teammate, "man on," "turn," "I got ball." Offense is characterized by visual or action communication, while defense has more voice usage. (However, **communication** is a must!).
- If you have cover on defense you can attack the ball. **Without cover you must delay**, give weak side help, stay goal side.
- Even long clearing should have an **intended receiver.** Almost all ball contacts (passes) must attempt to insure possession, with gambles taken in vicinity of goal in order to score.
- Use **feints to provide time** and space (turn away from pressure).
- Have intentions even before you receive a ball. Learn to visually check all around you on a regular basis. Try to work with your **head up** when in possession.

## PRINCIPLES OF COACHING
I. WARM-UP seven major soccer muscle areas.

II. Practice must be FUN (have some competitive activities, and/or fun activities).

III. CONDITIONING is part of every practice and can be done in conjunction with ball skills, techniques, tactics, etc.

IV. CHANGE activities as listed in program which has 5 basic activities in a given practice. Each part may have several wrinkles.

V. DEMONSTRATE and explain. Have the team do the exercise; correct, and continue. (Do not talk steadily; stop activity for 15-30 seconds, correct, then continue). Recreate the correct picture, allow a free pass or two for a clear picture and play resumes.

VI. Even though there is correction, the core behavior is PRAISE. Players are there because they want to be, so they MUST be doing well. If they are not, it is best to assume it's your problem (be it true or false) and that you can give them the correct level activity so success will be achieved; therefore praise is in order.

VII. SUCCESSFUL activity counts the most. Do not fear leaving an activity. Go to the rest of your plan; you might need time to think about why an activity did not go well.

VIII. Be sure the team has real INPUT. Listen and observe carefully. You will never stop being the leader as a coach, but great leaders know the needs, feelings, levels, etc. of those they lead; they learn what is needed from listening as well as observing, thinking, creating, etc.

IX. Technique (skills) must be UNIFIED to tactics and systems of play. Technique (skills) must be practiced by every one, (even professionals) because skills have a MAINTENANCE aspect as well as a learning aspect. After skills, come individual tactics, group tactics, and team tactics. Try to use the same skill in a scrimmage in a given team system of play. However, soccer thinking skills (tactics) must begin as early as age 6, though it may simply be a 1-2 movement, and all must be incorporated into a shortsided game.

X. THEMATIC PRACTICE. Attempt to relate areas of given practice to one basic skill. However, break it down to manageable components following the basic practice procedure (steps one through five).

Only correct practice is valuable; when players are too tired or too disinterested, stop and rest or change to another activity. Poor repetitions are counter productive. Proper repetition develops excellence. Guide line: 40% or more incorrect repetitions demands a change. 95% or more correct repetitions may be a sign the activity is too easy and therefore possibly boring.

Xl. Use a clearly developed **progression** from attaining technical quality to using the skill in a match related (shortsided game) situation.

## SAMPLE PRACTICE SEQUENCE #A
## POWER INSTEP KICK-SHOOTING (keeping balls low)
### 1. WARM-UP AND STRETCHING
Dribble ball for pre-stretch warm-up. Stretch all seven basic muscle areas. Warm-up having groups of 4 play keep-away, three maintaining possession, one defends, and as drill is in progress let players move out from 8 yards apart to 15 yards and use the instep kick pass.

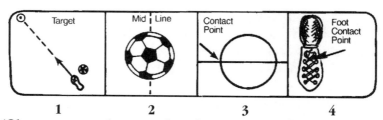

(Observe errors players make when using instep kick).

### II. TECHNIQUE
Teach the instep kick:
- Emphasize correction of technique observed in warm-up drill.
- Ankle locked, toe down.
- Non-kicking foot facing target and on side of ball a little distance away. Diagram #1.
- Eye on exact place of kicking (midline of ball). Diagram #2.

- Strike center slightly above the midpoint (strike the top half of the ball. Have players touch the correct spot on the ball.) Diagram #3.
- Head down and steady—see foot hit through the ball.
- Identify proper place on footwear that should contact the ball (center of shoe laces preferred) with a very slight turning in of the foot. Diagram #4.
- Follow through so that non-kicking foot is lifted from the ground and player lands on kicking foot.
- Demonstrate the knee lift by striking a ball 4 or 5 times that is held in place (medicine ball useful for showing this). Knee over ball for low trajectory.
- In shooting, accuracy comes first, then power.
- Encourage players to use their hands for body balance.
- Demonstrate complete kick.

Stress only 1 or 2 points at first. Not all in one day. Players practice in pairs (one or two pairs working on goal—change and rotate periodically). Make corrections of individuals. Stop practice and correct the major (most common observed) fault. Generally the biggest problem players have is striking the top half of the ball in order to keep the shot low which is a result of not getting the knee over the ball.

Players continue practicing the technique.

Continue practice with ball rolling slowly toward the player (be certain the balls are still being shot low); also continue kicks with a one touch dribble. Increase difficulty appropriate to your players—balls from the side,with a bounce, receive-turn-shoot, etc.

Add:Receiver moves when the player is three paces away from kicking the ball and the kicker must still send ball in the correct direction (simulates adjusting to keeper's move or a moving receiver).

## III. GROUP TACTICS

Make groups of approximately five players—one goalie defending the goal. Other groups use the flexible corner flags for goals (ones that do not fall when hit; obstacle course markers). Have one defender and three attackers who set up one person for a 15-20 yards power instep shot on goal. Be sure to follow your shot. Above age 12 this may be more appropriate with 3 v 2 instead of 3 v 1. For more advanced players instead of one dribble and the shot, or a ball rolling toward them, you can add square ball instep power shot. Players who are very advanced can use swerves, but they must call out how shot will swerve, in or out, before execution. Have players only use their non-dominant foot (righties use left foot) for four or five minutes. Be certain the shots are still low; if not, stop and explain how the low shot has to be gone down to while the up shot is played to the height of the goal keeper's hands. Keeper is already erect and therefore requires little effort for a save.

## IV. SPECIAL SITUATIONS

Coordinated Sample - Offensive Indirect Free Kick.

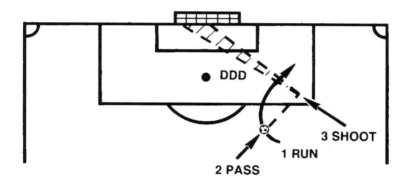

In general, keep restarts simple with few passes as possible to reduce chances of error.

Use your own favorite set play. After play is set up and understood, consider two groups. Have no less than one attempt 30 seconds—hopefully more. Obviously, there is incidental defensive free-kick practice occurring. Player one fakes shot and runs wide, player two passes it to three, player three shoots a hard instep shot with an attempt to see where the opening in the goal is. If player number one is unattended, ball can go to number one and he can shoot. It is often best to have the team divided into two separate groups so there are more attempts. Everyone should get one or two chances to do the shooting, with the players who will actually do this in a game getting extra opportunities. The coach can drop the ball anywhere and see how fast the defense can set up or how fast the offense can set up. Only call out who will kick it when the ball is set up. This should be a fast moving drill.

## V. GROUP TACTICS

Team shortsided play, but the defense will be passive within three or four yards of the penalty box line (shaded areas) so that offensive players can have much practice taking power instep shots.

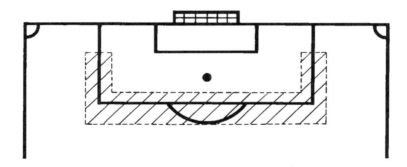

Any time ball is in shaded area the defense should relax to allow much long distance shooting.  Another way is to set up two half field groups with a goalkeeper, two defenders, and four or five attackers. Simply rotate positions periodically. This is also good practice for the keeper.  No practice is complete without shooting on goal with some pressure. Therefore, increase the pressure by allowing more defensive pressure everywhere, or even increase the number of defenders. Of course, every practice requires a goal with a net.  Another method is to 4 v 4 to full sized goals in 50 X 50 yard area and have neutral players support the offensive team.

Another possibility is to have 3 v 3 with 2 players who are always on the offensive team.

All of these situations will facilitate many shots on goal.

## SAMPLE PRACTICE SEQUENCE - #B
## Heading - Emphasis on Turning Ball and Keeping It Down.

### I. WARM-UP AND STRETCHING

Play 4 v 2, then stretch all seven basic muscle areas using pairs.

### WARM-UP WITH BALL

Dribble activity with commands called out; stop, backwards, forward, etc. Dribble MAKING BELIEVE you are picking up grass, feint dribble with outside of foot, go left, swing your arms, simulate heading a ball, shuffle sideways, skip, jump, somersault, etc. Do some juggling which emphasizes heading since that is the lesson of the day.

### II. INDIVIDUAL TECHNIQUE

For young children a pendulum header T-bar is helpful, or one or two pendulum balls hung from a goal, or serves from very close (4 feet). Emphasis: proper contact location--forehead near hair line—at the curvature of the skull (skull is thickest there). The pendulum devices slow up the ball and make proper instruction easier, but a good job can be done if attention is given to proper serving. ..(though you can never achieve the number of repetitions for a given time period as when you have a pendulum device). The ball in full free flight from long distances at early stages encourages eye closing, and what we really want is eyes opened. Have more advanced players turn the ball 90°. Therefore, it is best to have 3 people in a group—header, server and receiver. Ball should bounce at the receiver's feet. Demonstrate how by going up, pitching head down and slightly sideways, and making contact with top half of the ball that you can get the ball to go down, which inevitably is a nightmare for the keeper to save. Shots taken with the head use the flat portion of the forehead.

Clearing

Shooting

If players are not establishing height, this is a problem. This is where the pendulum device can force players to jump up. The T-Pendulum Heading device is very good because you can set one side at a height for the taller players. Try to get players to at least make contact with top half of ball when it is 12" above their heads while standing on their toes. Obviously advanced players should be able to go much higher. Be certain to challenge your players jumping ability. See if players can use the arm thrust and neck snap. The back curvature is a must. Order of priority: accurate direction; establishing height; power (high ball velocity).

Let server get farther away, maintaining proper location, eyes opened, and ball being TURNED. If goal is available have one or two pairs working the drill in the goal area. Rotate groups for use of goal. Have players jump over cardboard boxes or gates for establishing height.

### III. GROUP TACTICS

Put a keeper in the goal and have a 3 v 1 defender situation. For young players while the three are attacking the goal (or the make-shift obstacle course flag goals) player number 1 suddenly picks up a ball and hand serves it for a shot to number 2. Number 2 tries to score a header goal to open area of goal and to the ground forcing the keeper to a low dive.

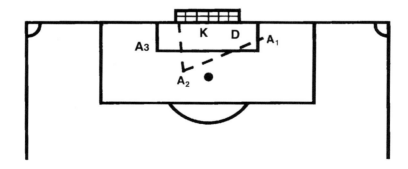

Chances for shots occur at random though everyone gets a chance to be an attacker.

Variations: 3 v 2, 4 v 2, 3 v 1 but ball kicked to shooter instead of served by hand; 6 v 4, no keeper and ball is lifted by kicking. Make any adjustments necessary to achieve a level where it is not something players could do without instruction nor is it so hard as to be overly frustrating or impossible. Instruction is usually challenging but players can achieve results with hard work.

## IV. SPECIAL SITUATIONS

Use your corner kick play. Some coaches prefer many people out of the box with a player going near post, another far post, another going just inside the penalty line, with others prepared for kicking shots or feeding head balls to the head of the three positions indicated.

Use one or two defenders and four or five strikers. Have a player hand-serve balls to the open man for a turning head shot.

Variations: eliminate server and have balls kicked in from corner; add defenders. For accuracy emphasis, use two keepers with no other defenders.

## V. TEAM TACTICS

6 v 6, 8 v 8, scrimmage, but in any case call for a corner kick every three minutes, even though no situation calling for one occurred.

Variations: Call for one from left corner and one from right each time there is a corner kick. Stress heading technique.

## SAFETY

Have players bring a drink to practice. Large mouth squirt bottles are convenient for this purpose, especially since they can be frozen or receive ice cubes. For hot weather water is the preferred drink. Electrolytes can be diluted (1-2 parts water) to make them acceptable.

First aid courses are advised and having a first aid kit is a definite. It is best for matches of youth groups to have a qualified parent responsible for this (possibly a nurse). It relieves the coach, gets parents involved, and hopefully responsibility will reduce negative yelling and irresponsibility. Youth coaches should make an effort to take a first aid course.

## EQUIPMENT

Over a period of time serious play requires equipment. Required equipment includes a goal with net affixed, obstacle course flags, cones, scrimmage vests, first aid kit, and a ball for each player (players can bring their own). Other equipment might be a pendulum header unit or two pendulum balls to hang from a goal, 5-aside goals, skill balls, a soccer medicine ball, whistle, and stop watch.

## YOUTH CLUB

One or two alternate (assistant) coaches should be prepared to do a practice. After all, youth coaching is a hobby with job responsibilities necessitating priority. However, player practices should almost never be cancelled (and need not if others are prepared to fill in). The game and the ball are a great teacher; after a brief warm-up the adult supervisor merely needs to be present for shortsided games.  The reason practice should not be cancelled is because there will be reasons why players must miss practice (illness, etc.). Seldom will there be 100% attendance.

Hopefully the head coach can make at least four of five scheduled practices and hopefully all players will be present for at least one practice per week.

Fitness is an aid to safety.

Game playing safety demands that players have had practice. Please recall that it is near impossible to instruct or improve players during contests. What little can be done is when players are on the sidelines. If not involved in play, a very simple, single idea might be handled.

Talking to a player with the ball or involved with play is destructive. Therefore, practice is really when the preponderance of teaching is accomplished. Game experience is needed, but without instruction in practice, players' growth is very restricted.

# Appendix vi
# Match Behavior & Analysis

The major function for a coach during matches as well as practice is that of a role model. Therefore the coach must exhibit self-control, poise, patience, and a positive sportsman-like attitude. The coach cannot be the players' mind, referee, and cheerleader. Constant talking, screaming, and berating are counterproductive. The coach needs to concentrate on WHAT is going well and poorly in the game. Then he must determine WHY. It is not enough to treat the symptoms. He/she must observe the game analytically, and identify the one or two major areas for change or improvement.

The great performance of any half time talk should be in regard to what the team did to prepare for the match on hand.

Before the game, a moment with each player individually can be very effective. The coach should learn which motivation techniques work for each player. The fiery emotional speech is not usually geared to soccer, since many players need to be more relaxed in order to make the right tactical decisions and technical executions. The coach who exhibits confidence, not cockiness, and has a prepared game plan does more for a team than one who depends upon rally cries and gimmicks.

Communication is the key to motivation; the coach must make sure that the players know what to do, and that they have practiced doing it in match-like situations. The players should know whether they are to play high or low pressure, man-to-man or zonal defense, attack from the middle or wings, and so forth.   During the first half, the coach should identify the team's major areas of strength and weakness. A good starting point would be the basic principles of attack and defense. Is there penetration, support, and mobility on attack? Is there delay (pressure on the ball), cover, and balance on defense? Is there quick transition? How were goals scored?

Halftime belongs to the players; the reason for halftime is to give the players a break from the continuous action of the game. The coach should allow the players that break before talking to them. As players come off the field, steer them away from the distractions of parents and friends. Listen to what they are saying to each other! Treat any injuries, and make sure that they all get water. Let them relax; comfort those who need reassurance. Then, and only then, will they be ready for instruction and preparing plans for the second half. The coach's half time remarks should focus on the one or two major problems in attack and defense, confining statements to general behavior, not individual players. A good approach with older players is to ask them where the team performed well and where they need improvement, then try to solve the problem together. Wrap up the talk with concise solutions to the major problems. The only effective solutions are those that have been realistically practiced. Again, individual attention is always a good motivator and can target exactly on what is needed for a given individual.

After the game, exchange handshakes with the other coach and have the players do the same with the other team. Move players to a quiet, safe environment, especially after a tough game. Give a very short summary of the game (half a minute), check for injuries, and announce the day and time of the next meeting. Following is a suggested list of questions to help the coach analyze the game. It is by no means complete, but it does offer a starting point.

### Attack: Do we have

### Penetration?
where   how   ground/air   pass/dribble   direct/indirect
safety/risk   passing ball/passing responsibility
individual/team   exploitation of opponents' weakness
beat offside trap

## Support?

| where | how | width/depth | close/far |
|---|---|---|---|
| combination play | | always ready to receive | |
| with time & space/without time & space | | confusing defense | |
| fluid movement/rigid positions | | overloads | |
| overlaps | good timing | numbers up | |

## Mobility?

| where | how | width/depth | close/far |
|---|---|---|---|
| combination play | | accelerate to receive | |
| with time & space/without time & space | | | |
| fluid movement/rigid positions | | spread defense | |
| overloads | overlaps | good timing | |

## Transition?

| quick/slow | | whole team/part of team |
|---|---|---|
| recovery runs | strikers | defenders |
| midfielders | | keeper |

## Defense: Do we have

## Delay?

pressure on the ball
loose marking/tight marking
protecting space behind
forcing square or back passes
keeping attacker from turning & looking up
shepherding
tackling when there is cover
patience
chase from front runners
safety/risk

## Cover?

priority over marking
depth
cutting out passes
talk
freeback freer to cover
what third of the field

## Balance?

concentration
restricting space
cutting out passes
staying goal side
protecting space
talk
able to see both man & ball
numbers up

## Transition?

quick/slow
whole team/part of team
when to play all out defense
all out offense
only concentrate on defense when we are ahead of 2 goals

## Tactical Considerations

man-to-man/zonal defense
score/high pressure/low pressure defense
4-3-3/4-2-2
offside trap
how were goals scored
is there a mismatch
where is attacking space available
which techniques are helping/hurting
how are we losing the ball
are we exploiting opponent's weakness
are there any anticipated developments
is the weather, field, or environment a factor

## Personnel Considerations
is there leadership
is there teamwork
is keeper in command of area
which players are having problems
are they technical, tactical, or motivational problems
is everyone getting a chance to play

## Coach's Personal Considerations
**Am I:**
setting a good example
prepared
in control
showing respect
aware of player's psychological state
letting players decide what to do
observing objectively
setting realistic goals
positive
concerned with the way the team is playing or just the score
expecting players to do things that they haven't practiced
maintaining my sense of humor

# *Appendix vii*
# *Bibliography of Recommended Books, Journals, and Tapes*

**Books**
de Boer, Klass; *Indoor Soccer.*
Caruso, Andrew; *Soccer Coaching Ages 12-20*
Caruso, Andrew; *Soccer's Dynamic Shortsided Games*
DiCiccio, Tony; *Goalkeeping Medicine Ball Training.*
*Dutch Soccer Drills.* Masters Press, 1996
Hughes, Charles; *Soccer Tactics and Skills.* London, 1980
Machnik, Joseph & Frans Hoek; *So Now You Are A Goalkeeper.* New Haven: Phoenix Press, 1985.
Maher, Alan; *Complete Soccer Handbook.* New York: Parker Publishing Company, 1983.
Malone, Chris S.; *Safe Coaching*
McGettigan, James P.; *Winning Soccer Drills.*
Reese, Roy; *Manual of Soccer Coaching.*
Wade, Alan; *Coaching Strategies* (also several other titles)
Waiters, Tony; *Coaching Soccer Series.*
Warren, William; *Coaching and Motivation.*
Soccer Industry Council of America (SICA) has compiled an elaborate book that helps a group develop a multi field complex. SICA is part of the SGMA (Sporting Goods Manufactures of America) located at West Palm Beach, Florida. Excellent resource guide.

**Print Media**
*Soccer America*; Clay Berling, editor. P.O. Box 23704, Oakland, CA 94623 415-549-1414.
*Soccer Journal*; The National Soccer Coaches Association of America: Tim Schum, editor. West Gymnasium, SUNY Binghamton, Binghamton, NY 13901 607-777-2133.

**Videotapes**

Ajax; *The Ajax Trainging Method.*

Bonetti, Peter; *Goalkeeping Drills.*

Coerver, Wiel; *Soccer Fundamentals* (series of three tapes on basic techniques, beating an opponent, and shooting).

Hughes, Charles; *Soccer Tactics and Skills*
(series of seven tapes on creating space, attack, set plays, passing & support shooting, defending, and goalkeeping) .

KNVB; *The Dutch 4 v 4 Training Method.*

Shattuck, Jape. International Tactics Series (series of 5 tapes on individual and Group Tactics).

The Tactical Game. 1996 five tape tactical series.

van Balkom, Frans; *On the Attack* (series of three tapes on fast footwork and feinting, dribbling skills and drills, and shooting and heading).

van Gaal, Louis; *The Dutch Soccer School.*

Welsh, Alex; *Goalkeeping.*

*Any of the above mentioned Books and Videos can be purchased from REEDSWAIN, INC., Books and Videos. To Order Call 1-800-331-5191.*